WaterSource Press™

Presents

Torchwood
Calliope

Tribute to a Joyful Life

Best Wishes!

[signature]

Captain
Jeffrey L. Bair

Torchwood Calliope is a trademark of **WaterSource Press™**

All scripture quotations, unless otherwise indicated, are taken from the New King James Version®, Copyright © 1982 by Thomas Nelson, Inc. Used by permission. All rights reserved.

Cover illustration Cindy Bair, composition WaterSource Press™. Black and white refers to the duality of good (light) versus bad (darkness); a long narrow path lit by the Sword of Spirit, which is The Word of God, Ephesians 6:17 (King Richard's third crusade grip, hilt and blade with Joan of Arc's cruciform pommel), inscribed *In Omnia Paratus* (In All Things Prepared).

ISBN 978-0-9798222-0-9

Library of Congress Catalog Card Number

Published by WaterSource Press™
www.WaterSourcePress.com

Send inquiries to:
WaterSource Press
PO Box 6364
Bloomington, IL 61702-6364

Printed in the United States of America. In God We Trust.

About the Author

The author received a Master of Arts Degree through South Dakota State University in Political Science. He completed 32 additional graduate hours of study in Educational Administration, Educational Methods, and Technology Education at Illinois State University. He received a Bachelor of Applied Arts and Science Degree in Occupational Education from Texas State University. He received an Associate Degree in Digital Electronics Technology from the Community College of the Air Force. He is a certified Illinois Vocational Education Teacher in Industrial Arts.

The author served nearly twenty years in the United States Military. His duties and responsibilities included: Commander (in various capacities up to base level support), Operations (nuclear missile launch, command and control, special operations), Executive Officer (to the Commander of Air Rescue Service/Air Weather Service), Maintenance (cryptographic digital equipment, electromechanical devices, nuclear and aircraft systems), Military Training Instructor (Drill, Discipline and Military Studies).

The author served as an Industrial Technology high school teacher, receiving awards for model learning systems, and inspirational teaching methods. He served as an Education and Learning consultant for the State of Illinois. His students achieved high honors in a statewide engineering project, nominated him for teacher of the year, placing his name in *Who's Who Among American Teachers.*

He is currently an Industrial Technologist, having served the inventors of bar code and point of sales technologies, the largest print communications company in North America, and a pioneering company, experts in the packaging industry. He is a freelance consultant for corporate education, legislative affairs and small business administration.

Contents

The Contents of our lives are fleeting presents wrapped in close pasts tied up with future strings. Author

The *Contents* may be my favorite pages because they contain the summary of titles which in one confluence judge this work and its author. These titles, ideas, rhyme, composition and power of the pen give me reason to praise our merciful Father in Heaven. He truly inspires joy.

Preface

The *Torchwood Calliope* is a marvelous, whimsical, melodious machine. It speaks a universal language of music built on notes, tempo, timing, and sound. The calliope will delight your emotions with its golden pitched music and lighten your heart with its flame, if only you choose to look and listen.

Torchwood is an exotic resinous tree found in Florida and the West Indies. Its wood is used to make torches able to sustain a lit end, while the lumber is slowly consumed.

The Calliope is an American invention whereby steam flows through various adjusted whistles, causing a pleasant mellow toned tune. The whistles can be made of metals like copper, brass, or something plated (nickel, zinc, lead), and may be carved of hardwood or even made of plastic to create other types of tones. Though compressed air replaces the old steam power in the instrument among hobbyists today, hot vapor is still used to power a few large calliopes on riverboats.

Calliope was also the name of a Greek mythological goddess, meaning *beautiful–voiced*. She was the muse of epic poetry, daughter of Zeus and Mnemosyne. She is best known as Homer's muse of the Iliad and the Odyssey. In mythology, she was the oldest, wisest and most self-confident of the muses. Calliope was represented by a stylus and tablets. She wears a crown of gold and always carries writing utensils, book or a scroll.

Resonance is a powerful force in our universe. Some imagine the vibrations of a hidden energy hold the secret to combining the vastness of outer space with infinitesimal sub-atomic matter. Fire and sound coalesce to express energy on the face of conventional wisdom. We ponder with passion the value of great things and ideas, until metaphor bargains a truth with which we can reason. Here math, science and technology combine to demonstrate to the senses what poetry describes to our hearts and minds.

The notion in creating a *Torchwood Calliope* includes all these vibrant features mixed with imagination to suggest a man-made device extolling spirit, lyric, harmony, music, dexterity, fire, steam, energy, color, light, sound, resonance and many more ingredients from the human heart, mind and body. Neither *new age*, nor *self-awareness* models here. It's old, legendary, tried and true.

Find your place inside this dynamic momentum. Let apathy fade while you are attracted to *Torchwood's* fury like Old Glory snapping in the wind. Indifference will retreat as you are pulled into the elemental richness of lives lived, stories told and hope restored. Relationships will confide their commonality in you. Then timing, tempo, rhythm, and rhyme will grab your need for explanation in an unreasonable place or time, opening opportunity to ponder neglected ideas from ancient to present importance.

Finally, you will be able to express or convey ideas meant, but not easily told. As quality of expression extols our basic need for engendered spirit, the *Torchwood Calliope* exists in all of us. It is waiting to map a course powered by forces unseen yet real, upon the uncharted waters of our imaginations, while waves of glow-lit dreams and foaming desires of the heart illuminate a new direction.

Cast caution to the wind for a few moments of your hectic day and read about the *Torchwood Calliope*. Then see if you can feel the things described. It was a very barren place in which I penned the title verse for this grouping of ideas and memories. Yet every time I lifted the pen, the negative evaporated into a palatable peace, which provided a great strength. Toil became satisfying labor. Labor bore fruit the taste of which, I hope we never grow tired of savoring.

"We live in deeds, not years; in thoughts, not breaths; in feelings, not figures on a dial. We should count time by heart-throbs. He most lives who thinks most, feels the noblest, acts the best. And he whose heart beats quickest lives the longest; lives in one hour more than do some in years, whose fat blood sleeps as it slips along their veins. Life is but a means to an end; that end, beginning, mean, and end to all things – God.
The dead have all the glory of the world."

Philip James Bailey
(1816-1902)
English Poet

From: *Festus*

Guide to Dedications and Tributes:

If you share the things written or pass on some of the borrowed notions arranged in this book, then it meets its intended purpose. A message or a meaning put in a special way, aught to cause a significant emotional event for someone you care about. This was my reason for putting these pages together; to share meaningful experiences through a *Tribute to a Joyful Life*.

Now, if any of these verses, or perhaps the entire work appeals to you, please present them that way. Often, a simple dedication or tribute given to a person at a time that is just right for them, tells that person you know about their affections, and you understand their intuitions. This will present a gift greater than any you can buy.

Here are a few suggestions for dedicating all or a part of this book to a special someone:

First, you may decide to dedicate the entire book by using a blank space in the front or back. Also, consider each part of the book as a potential gift: dedicate and write to them at the beginning of each section. Short phrases can have big impact on someone's life.

Lastly, look at the verses, quotes and proverbs to write a specific dedication on a page facing the poem, prose or psalm you plan to compliment. Write any combination of heartfelt tributes from sections listed in the *Contents*. Use the blank space below my dedications for your own personalizations.

For instance...

I dedicate this poem to my wife, Abigail. You are my Angel sent just when I needed inspiration in life. Like the poet said, "...For when I needed you most, you were there."

Love Always,
John

Also, write dedications to yourself. Use this like a journal of inquiries you can return to often, and from which you can gather strength and encouragement.

Use calligraphy, a fountain pen, or any writing utensil you like. However, consider drafting your thoughts on paper first, or perhaps lightly penciling in the tribute before applying ink. This will add a nice, thoughtful, permanence to your gift, which will last a lifetime. By adding personal tributes to this collection of verse and rhyme, you give and will receive in return the greatest gift of all—Love with Understanding.

"I wish all our clever young poets would remember by [plain] definitions of prose and poetry; that is, prose equals words in their best order; poetry equals the *best* words in the *best* order."

**Samuel Taylor Coleridge
(1772-1834)
English poet**

Author of *The Rime of the Ancient Mariner,
and Kubla Khan*

Bound with love for...

Becky, Analiesa, Vanessa, Nicholas, Senja, Abigail, Lauren, Silas, Adam and Riley.

Introduction

E very book needs a theme. So, I chose the light and sound of this first poem to lead for its unusual composition. It spearheads a collection of verse, rhyme and thoughts to inspire imagination. Temporal metaphor and simple poetry, describe a place and time we need to consider in relieving anxiety, fear and tension. Once relaxed, our thoughts can move about freely with passion, for knowing the essence of God.

I wrote the poem *Torchwood Calliope* in 1993 while supporting the Desert Storm task force in Saudi Arabia. During this time, I fasted, prayed and concentrated on spiritual subjects. You might wonder how reading scripture in a desert could influence such a whimsical verse.

I'm not sure, but I remember praying for inspiration to find words which communicate my absolute *joy in life* to people whom I hold dear. Somehow, music and motion became a notion, then a view of a flaming steam calliope. I believe God has a light-hearted wit because our spirits are complimented by good humor, and He wants His people to make a joyful noise to give Him praise and glory.

The desert is a dry, barren wasteland and it reminds us of how helpless we are without the special provisions of a loving Creator. Our physical weakness without proper cover in such a harsh setting—stifling heat, lack of hydration in a talcum dust aridity, and fear of such critters as large black scorpions and huge ants with long spider-like legs, suggests less joy is expected. Yet, it was just this type of environment that opened a new way of thinking or perceiving God's blessings that fostered the light and sound of the *Torchwood Calliope* to persist in my mind's eye.

Part 1 begins the journey with motivation for seeking a joy filled life—family, friends and fulfillment. The realization that family satisfies our basic duty in life, comes as a soft persistent pelting through observing happiness in others. God's intention for our existence and for following His rules are rejected by ever changing culture, until an individual need for His resolve forces us back to Him.

Part 2 describes hard lessons learned upon the wide road of life. It conveys darkness, desires of the flesh, and the search for understanding trials of human nature and political principles. Please consider the ease with which one can fall, drowning in the rushing river current of common cultural reasoning that encourages bad behavior with contempt for being saved—all for the sake of entertainment.

Part 3 is about soft lessons of heart and mind. It is the focus group for correcting misplaced efforts and wasted energy. This section begins the healing process by first concentrating on the *Big Three* technologies of spirit, which prepare us for all understanding and action. It gives examples of these elemental properties to prove their worth and utility in forming a joyful life.

Part 4 gets serious from a warrior's perspective. These verses, narratives, proverbs and quotes provide the mettle from which the authority to succeed over powers and principalities originates. Not for the faint of heart, this part records hopeless battles joined with impossible victories won through powers unseen and faith alone relied upon.

Part 5 completes the journey by recalling the importance of life-long-learning. In the end, the student and the teacher become one. Through my personal experience, I share the truth about student-teacher relations, and describe the wonder in seeking knowledge of *how* our universe works without supplanting faith in Creation.

I cannot take you to the desert. You have not gone with me through all the battles and experiences this life-time of joy has produced. However, if you are willing to read the verses, quotes and paragraphs in this book, you will begin to see things in a new light and hear small voices of reason that only come to a mind attuned to resonance in wisdom.

So, hold on to your way of thinking as each wave the *Torchwood Calliope* lifts up and over, buffets your mood and understanding. In the course of human endeavor, we are constantly prodded by an unseen force, which begs our mind to question, "Why?"

It took some grim trials, mind and body numbing tribulations, and many sweet victories to convince me of the following notions. I hope you enjoy the ride along-side my memories and contemplations. If you do, be advised the ship is built of sturdy timbers. The experiences will pitch and yaw like eclectic variations in a first heard symphony. Some intonations will sound familiar; others must be revisited to allow your own experiences to absorb their meaning.

Anyone can mount a broken horse. It takes real courage to trust a Maverick. So come along for a ride—if you dare!

He said, "I'm looking for a philosopher that will give me contentment."
I asked, "What about Jesus?"
He said, "I'm still looking for the star..."

Conversation with a successful businessman
At a stockholders' meeting, October 2006
Midtown Manhattan, NY

Part 1

Pursuing Joy
Colored Leaves Around the Tree

Part 1 of this book is a collection of verse worth visiting from time to time. During the hustle of life, we tend to harden our hearts against harmonious, lyrical and poetic matter. We darken our view of the world with work or school related issues, sense-filled pleasures, instant gratification and material objects.

These things can blot out the truth, joy and life that God wants us to live. We are aware of our faults and of something missing, but we choose to cover the void with weak popular opinion, worthless trivia and entertaining distractions.

Reach out and take hold of *Part 1*. Put yourself in each poem. Try to find a fit for someone you care about. Then share the poem with them. Allow yourself to wonder through these pages. There are messages here from the ages for you, family and friends.

Cracks in concrete consciousness broke open under the pressure of my pen and words bubbled up, flowing onto the pages like paint drying on canvas, into a portrait of living. If you find anything in these verses to light a spark within your heart, then read on.

If the hard shell of *just existing* begins to melt a little, be sure to enjoy its release. Then pour into a gentler state of mind for awhile and relax with its effects. It is sweet cherry-flavored medicine for the heart, mind and soul.

We begin with family matters and progress through our treatment of others. Simple and desirable things can get complicated and seem unattainable. How do we act to insure a genuine compliment or gracious attitude comes our way? Sometimes age has a lot to do with it. Youngsters often have the advantage of receiving forgiveness for their mistakes. Yet, no matter what our age, we all need help with balancing power, prestige and purpose in our lives.

Where are the answers? How much is too much to own? When is it good to go easy on an offender of our personal space, possessions, or pride? I struggle with opportunities to be a good example to others, as I know you do. Taking the time to consider issues of a less popular nature might just open our eyes to new life. Is that too much to consider, or absurd enough to stop right here and go no further?

Will we try once more to suffer a message in hope of hitting something of real value? The thing about hunting for treasure is that sometimes the chest opens laden with gold, jewels and curious notions. Other times we never find a chest, or it is eaten away by decay to impart an edifice once held as triumphant, but is now passé. Without the hunt, we live in mediocrity; too afraid of finding lost treasure because we wouldn't know what to do with it, or just terrified of change.

Should *Part 1* touch a curious emotion, don't be embarrassed, press forward. There is a slight bump in the road ahead. But then, that's what bumps are for: to carry us up and over underlying swells of the unknown, on a journey we dare not miss, through a forest of uneasy calm, riding in a surrey of favored notion and wistful resolve; unsure of the destination, yet certain of purpose.

"Every day you may make progress. Every step may be fruitful. Yet there will stretch out before you an ever-lengthening, ever-ascending, ever-improving path. You know you will never get to the end of the journey. But this, so far from discouraging, adds to the joy and glory of the climb."

Sir Winston Churchill (1874 - 1965)
Great Britain Prime Minister
World War II

Part 1 Dedication

I dedicate Part One to Rebecca, my beautiful wife. She prepared the table of inspiration, bore the pain and sacrifices of inviting all our children to join us for the banquet of life, and never once desired anything more than love in return.

I Love You Dear,
Jeff

Commit your works to the Lord,
and your thoughts will be established.

Proverbs 16:3

Torchwood Calliope Narrative

Torchwood Calliope is my fiercest enterprise penned under the rigors of four months in Saudi Arabia serving as a Command and Control Operations Officer with the United States Air Force. I lived in Khobar Tours with hundreds of other G.I.s from all branches of the military. We deployed and worked in a foreign land to help insure the peace and prosperity of others at home. In my spare time, I read Charles Dickens' *Pickwick Papers*, various classical poetry, a contemporary history-based fictional novel, and the Holy Bible.

I attended worship services with a few comrades in an underground parking garage converted into a chapel. We virtually hid our faith because it's illegal to show any signs or speak of an outside religion in Saudi Arabia. We sang hymns along with recorded organ music—kind of like holy karaoke. These were the most poignant religious services I ever attended.

I stayed to myself, fasting, praying, and meditating. I wrote letters to my wife and children mailing gifts of 18-carat gold and silver to them. In return, they sent more valuable gifts in the form of cookies, cereal, and videotaped family messages.

The chow hall food was bad in this place, tap water undrinkable and more than one tenuous moment kept things interesting. Once, there was an explosion in a dormitory that blew a hole in the floor and ceiling of a concrete apartment. It wiped out the living space and damaged the rooms above and below. I was walking to chow when the smoke could be seen coming from one of the windows. Things were never quite as they were supposed to seem in that place.

We heard there were no casualties and that Saudi maintenance men fixing leaky hot water heaters caused the explosion. We were told they took out the pressure safety valves and replaced them with solid plugs. Nothing more was said. And we wondered whose apartment would blow up next.

I worked 12 hour shifts, jogged the perimeter road and lifted weights to stay in shape. I had dysentery from the day after I arrived until I returned home. This malady was so common that the medics placed stomach and diarrhea medicine in baskets on their office counter for self-service.

Stark reminders of Desert Storm were near us. The parking lot outside my building was once a multistory dwelling damaged, with several casualties and deaths during the first Gulf War, by a SCUD missile attack. In 1996, after my stay was over, a truck bomb destroyed the dormitory where one of my friends and his troops were staying. His life was spared with only a leg injury, but he suffers from mental anguish over the death and injuries of his troops. I ask God for His mercy and pray for the souls lost, the survivors' mental health and for all their families.

Today these losses and sacrifices are eclipsed by the devastating cost in lives, limbs, families and human spirit lost in the effort to rebuild Iraq and Afghanistan; worthy goals, requiring constant assessment by good and wise people.

While in Saudi Arabia, I visited local shops and toured the area quite a bit. I drove through the city once by myself for a personal view of life there. I saw some beautiful homes and mosques. The locals seemed friendly. While visiting a small village some distance away, I had the impression of stepping back in time 2000 years.

There were modern touches of Western civilization, which contrasted with irony the ancient brick forts turned into holy places nearby. Five broadcast prayers a day from towers, traditional Arab clothing and the endless barren desert combined to impress easily another time in one's mind.

I was struck by the notion that Jesus of Nazareth worked under similar conditions. His country was occupied by a foreign empire that supported severe penalties for even suggesting religious differences and practices. Jesus Christ was very brave. His followers were too.

We were still bombing Baghdad with security threats always present. Intimidation in the open-air markets and while on tours was mostly an unintelligible verbal haranguing from a robed cleric with waving hand gestures, hosted by an armed guard (especially when our female troops were present and more so during Ramadan). Yet, I found the common people charming and their children curious and respectful. We had no idea a billionaire Saudi prince wished us all dead.

Torchwood Calliope is the product of prayer. Every time I read it, I am transported to another place. I believe it was God's gift to lift my spirits in a strange and barren land.

"It's the unconquerable soul of man, not the nature of the weapon he uses, that insures victory."

**General George S. Patton, Jr.
(1885-1945)**

American Soldier

Torchwood Calliope Dedication

I dedicate this poem to my brothers and sisters in Christ who need to hear and see the Spirit, and feel alive in the wilderness.

Respectfully Yours,
Jeff Bair

Great is my boldness of speech toward you.
Great is my boasting on your behalf.
I am filled with comfort.
I am exceedingly joyful in all our tribulation.

2 Corinthians 7:4

Torchwood Calliope

Melodious Calliope,
    Crescent pipes peel.
Flutes vibrant shrill, mix tenor 'till,
    Brass tones congeal.
Magical tune, big bass bassoon,
    Reeds alto chime;
        Nickel plate piccolo rhyme.

Boards weather worn, bowed planking shorn,
    Paint layered thick.
Large yellow pipe, spun cherry stripe,
    Piceous deck.
Cabinet white, glistening bright,
    Glazed pearl like glass;
        Great brattle shape shaking past.

Keys light as air, dance everywhere,
    Bellow pulls whirl.
Knobs pinwheel shape, flags made of crepe,
    Slowly unfurl.
Wide rainbow stripe, soars out of sight,
    'Round torchwood mast;
        Sails globose yank anchor cast.

Brown bellows flop, suck up and pop!
    Wet from cooled steam.
Tanned leather mops, spill over tops,
    Copper pipes green.
Toot whistle sweet, staccato beat,
    Thinks me of noon;
        Swiss cheese and bread snack-time tune.

Gold sparkle sound, sun setting down,
  Alto pipes hush.
Old baritone, passionate moan,
  Heart pounding rush.
Small candle lights, glow twilit pipes,
  Quick Spanish flair;
    Flame breaking out here and there.

Allegro blend, nearing the end,
  Tin horn seems trite.
Vortex of steam, moon mirror beam,
  Light neon night.
Cloud cover lit, curved angles fit,
  Under dark sky;
    Dream thee Calliope nigh.

Autonomous Narrative

My professional existence always seemed to be like a vocal expression held an octave below a dull scream. Author

A young man and woman are married in the summer of 1975. They first meet in kindergarten. Years later, they experience romantic liaison leading to a high school graduation wedding. As childhood friends, they used to play football in the streets of their neighborhood, but now plan a family together.

They have three beautiful children (two girls and a boy), and enter society as hard working, God fearing, tax paying citizens. From job changes, through career moves, they meet each new challenge and salary differential with courage and optimism. Sacrifice leads to security. Security leads to autonomy.

This poem was my first clear victory in verse. It took six months to write, but I wasn't finished until I fixed the second line several years later. I would wake up at 2:00 a.m. and work on it until a single idea was appropriately expressed. This was a labor of love for Rebecca, the love of my life.

"A true poem is distinguished not so much by a felicitous expression, or any thought it suggests, as by the atmosphere which surrounds it. Most have beauty of outline merely, and are striking as the form and bearing of a stranger; but true verses come toward us indistinctly, as the very breath of all friendliness, and envelop us in their spirit and fragrance."

Henry David Thoreau (1817-1862)
American philosopher, naturalist

Autonomous Dedication

I dedicate this poem to my beloved Becky. She should have chosen me for d*uck, duck, gray duck* in Kindergarten, but God worked it out in His time. So much rides on the winds of moments shared, as we are smaller than a speck in His plans. Yet, God allows us to think independent thoughts and look forward to autonomous days ahead. Hope remains alive while dreams survive.

Love always,
Jeff

Peace I leave with you, My peace I give to you;
not as the world gives do I give to you.
Let not your heart be troubled, neither let it be afraid.

John 14:27

Autonomous

Autumn's crimson colored crown,
　Cape lies creped on emerald gown.
Someday we will settle down,
　Autumn colors all around.

Now we hurry here and there,
　No time left for us to share.
Ambitions chase rainbow's end,
　Bright hues fade as oft' they tend.

If I only had my way,
　Autumn colors everyday,
Pastel yellow, red, and blue.
　Sacrifice the rainbow's hue,
　　When we live amid our autumn colored mood.

In the leisure of our ways,
　Turning hours into days.
Keeping silence shedding sounds,
　Autumn colored hush surrounds.

A gentler time spent with you,
　All the memories still to do.
Work relations now it seems,
　Guard our most elusive dreams.

If I only had my way,
　Autumn colors everyday.
Orange sails float freely by,
　Halo tipped in azure sky,
　　When we wish awhile our autumn colored mind.

Fragrant pine tree's needles play,
  Brown beneath their green bough sway.
Oak and maple leaves abound,
  Brightly painted on the ground.

Soon their colors turn to gray,
  Winter silver's on the way.
Like the rainbow's once bright hue,
  Tranquil breezes must ensue.

If I only had my way,
  Autumn colors everyday.
Burning leaves fall from the trees.
  Pastel colors blend with ease,
    When we live our dream, in autumn colored peace.

Promise Narrative

I began this poem easily but it was time consuming to polish. Long hours in a once active nuclear missile field, under the South Dakota prairie, afforded relative quite time to clean up my intended message.

The slow drone of a huge electric motor generator, buzzers and bells occasioning, and electromechanical printers monotonously *cachuncking,* interrupted me frequently. Yet, repetitive disciplined responses escorted high operational performance with intermittent spells of quiet enough to harness solemnity.

The verse was fashioned 60 to 90 feet below the earth's surface (depending on which of 15 Launch Control Centers I was in) at a constant 55 degrees Fahrenheit. We were dependent for the very air we breathed from above, pumped down to our subterranean battle zone that comprised the front lines of *The Cold War.* We were the world's first remote control warriors with Armageddon at our fingertips.

Missileers, with families, pondered the need to have their loved ones ready in a moments notice to leave the area should an incoming nuclear strike occur. I kissed my wife and children good-bye eight times a month for four years, knowing that they would not survive an attack. A strange veracity to life vexed our emotions between surreal strategic planning with battle tactics, and frequenting normalcy in a family environment.

The only insurance against the unthinkable horror of this unique warfare actually happening, was our deafening assurance to any aggressor that we would certainly devastate their homeland should they dare preempt an attack. After the *Evil Empire* collapsed, missile duty was over and I learned how certain they were we meant business and believed we could carry out our mission in case of their first strike. These were perilous times impressing fear in the hearts of all mankind. We risked annihilation on our adversary's sanity, with quiet reservation of our own.

This kind of duty places a life-long burden on those who take it seriously. We became experts in attention to detail, aficionados of perfection in operational actions, and compulsive achievers. To court these activities with the appropriate energy, mustering battle strength on a consistent basis, required absolute devotion to duty. It became habit. An outlet for releasing pent-up force was needed to maintain balance of heart, mind and body. Poetry was one relief valve for me.

Writing this poem gave way often to operational priorities. I was finishing a masters degree, doing Squadron Officers School by correspondence, presiding over staff projects, designing fund raising collectibles and new uniform items, constantly studying nuclear missile operations procedures, testing on codes, and planning my Launch Control Center upgrade. Off-duty I was crew chief on a successful racecar team. Winning the annual Grand Nationals added to strain. I calmed the urges of pride through reading and writing poetry. It was powerful remedy for a stress-filled mind.

The poetry had to be hidden. It was not an acceptable past time among warriors. To my chagrin, I found out years later that our finest leaders enjoyed reading, or writing poetry: Washington, Adams, Lincoln, Churchill, Reagan, and even George S. Patton, Jr. *(Old Blood and Guts)*, found solace in verse, rhyme and its powerful effect on gentling angst.

In perilous times, we often turn to Psalms in Bible verse or lyric to quiet our hearts and strengthen resolve. The thunder of battle and scorching of ears by fierce negative rhetoric requires a healthy dose of healing resonance in the form of quick, concentrated syllables. These absorb into the fiber of our spirit to soft-land the train wrecks of destiny, or quiet the fear of them.

The nuclear era asks history to mark and remember well the demons possessing frightened politics and persuasive intellect, which nearly cowered our great nation into subjectivity. We won a mighty victory over impending slavery, stopping the slow but steady encroachment of parasitic influence that would take our liberty and subject all Americans to a less worthy existence.

Today we take it all for granted, as we do after every hard-won American war. We are too eager to embrace foolish rhetoric that would have us believe evil collapses on its own. That cowering behind false logic and intellectual illusion will defeat any threat to our Liberty and Freedom.

I can never forget the critical tactics employed to defeat our Cold War adversaries, because God placed me at the center of the mêlée. In the middle of the storm, through prayer, an Angel touched my heart and out poured this *Promise*.

"The name of peace is sweet, and it is itself beneficial, but there is a great difference between peace and servitude. Peace is freedom in tranquility; servitude is the worst of all evils, to be resisted not only by war, but even by death."

**Cicero, Marcus Tullius
(106 - 43 BC)**

Roman author, orator, politician

Promise Dedication

I dedicate *Promise* to my long-suffering, self-sacrificing, ever-supportive bride. This verse I give to you as a heart felt thank you. I can never fully repay all the debts I owe you for loving and supporting me through thick and thin. But let me start with this *Promise*.

> Till the 12th of Never,
> Always Yours,
> Jeff

*Let your fountain be blessed and rejoice
with the wife of your youth.*

Proverbs 5:18

Promise

I remember the days you prayed for me,
  Enough wisdom, courage, serenity;
To fight pride, which tried, yours prayers to demise,
  Wished virtues: courageous, serene and wise.

As soft as the cloth you wept in alone,
  Dampened by tears so pain never shown.
The light in your eyes and love in your smile,
  Said belated dreams could wait for awhile.

My ship of high goals reckoned stars achieve,
  Navigate by faith in God, you believe.
Near capsize blew ignorant sails to learn,
  I found trust in you to ballast each turn.

When lean times came to our door, as they do,
  Never once did I hear complaint from you.
And when running low were new clothes and milk,
  You turned salt into butter, and rags to silk.

So fear not now as our journey eases,
  I'll provide and give whatever pleases.
Always I will love and protect you, Dear,
  For when I needed you most – you were there.

Princess Narrative

Analiesa was born at the end of our first year of marriage; we were both 19 years old. The product of love, she was an absolute blessing to us, and especially to her mother. My first tour of military service found us in Spangdahlem, Germany. It is a remote rural place in a foreign land, and I remember our youthful anxiety over leaving all the familiar things back home. Still, it was an exciting assignment.

I was a cryptographic electronics computer technician. Working the night shift mostly, I left my young wife alone in our tiny apartment located on Markt Strasse, in the small West German town of Speicher. Unable to drive a manual shift car, she stayed in our little apartment until I came home, or woke up, to take her and the baby for a ride. Occasionally she was brave enough to venture into the village to get bread. At the time, few people could or would speak English, and Becky was in no mood to learn the language.

The German countryside was like a picture out of a 19th century history book. The small plot farmers were using horse and oxen to plow their fields. Virtually all the surrounding farmland was planted in sugar beets. The produce was a cash crop and the green tops made a good feed for the oxen.

Poignant reminders of the Second World War were omnipresent. Two Sherman tanks were left out in a field perhaps by Patton's U.S. Third Army's march in the frozen winter to relieve Bastogne during the Battle of the Bulge. Large I-beam, tri-crossed tanks traps still lined small roads. *"Sieg Heil!"* emanated from a drunken veteran across a *gasthouse* bar room.

Yet, the most revealing part of the wars still near term influence was found in the stories told by our German landlord who, between his broken English and my basic German, expressed his time in a Russian P.O.W. camp.

It is not like that anymore. Jacob Heinz is gone now and southwest rural Germany is prospering with John Deere tractors and lawn mowers.

Analiesa kept her mother busy for weeks at a time during my absences at technical schools. Then, we all shared three enjoyable months together in Latina, Italy while I was in a NATO training environment. Analiesa (Pooky) was only a year old. Cute as a new holiday penny, she stole a lot of attention from acquaintances. She learned to take her first steps on the marble floor in our Italian flat.

Back in West Germany, times were very difficult for my wife especially when our car was broken and I couldn't afford to fix it for three months. She stayed in our little apartment for weeks on end, while I hitchhiked to work and brought groceries home on a small, old motorcycle.

I know Pooky kept her mother from leaving me alone in Europe. Children are certainly blessings to a marriage in more ways than we can measure.

"The greatest part of our happiness or misery depends on our dispositions, and not on our circumstances."

Martha Washington
(1731 – 1802)

First American Lady

Princess Dedication

I dedicate *Princess* to my first daughter Analiesa, who earned the title of Princess by patiently tolerating my mistakes as a new father. She is a woman with a big heart and burning desire to serve others as teacher and mentor. God bless each step of your walk on the narrow path as He shows you the lamp lit trail of Life.

I love you,
Dad

She is the tree of life to those who take hold of her,
and happy are all who retain her.

Proverbs 3:18

Princess

Sonorous song sing! True tale be told,
  Of a princess once lived in this land.
Warm charming ways, toll loudly and bold,
  The ring of this Belle, graced on her hand.

Legend would write, Princess Rella Belle,
  No other in this land lived as fair.
With milk chocolate eyes, and hair they tell,
  Silken to touch, layered soft as air.

Yet, her beauty told much more than this,
  Beyond complexion, her soul ran deep.
While knights challenged each other for her kiss,
  Only one knew her love safe to keep.

His message was strong, simple and sure,
  Touch not this lady's heart dare.
For none knew love more faithful or pure,
  Than the lady and husband did share.

All those who approached their love could see,
  Between Belle and her beau for all time.
Never before has been, nor ever shall be,
  A love greater than this tale doth rhyme.

Angel Star Narrative

Angel Star was written during a time of intense prayer for guidance on rearing teenagers in a material humanistic environment. Vanessa, our second child, was born a bundle of pure delight. She has a heart as big as the moon. Like most children, she searched for her place in the spotlight and once there, she found modesty, virtue, reason, discipline and a host of other good qualities.

I particularly appreciate her patience with me during the years of her young life when I missed school plays, parties, tears and smiles. I know I cannot make up for the lost moments or regain the unrepeatable memories. We all endured these difficult sacrifices so our freedom, security and prosperity could be guarded. Children need help with these concepts, as each adult generation must go off to war.

I have boundless pride in this young woman for sharing the burden of sacrifice at an early stage in her life. Having withstood the worst of this tyranny, she arrived safe home through the storms, on platinum sails, guided to a protected harbor by a white dove.

We all play our piece on the stage called life. Some parts play better than others do and not all receive the same payback or applause. My reward came in the form of an *Angel Star*, more than I ever deserved or could have hoped for in a child.

**"All the world's a stage,
And all the men and women merely players..."**

**William Shakespeare
(1564-1616)**

Angel Star Dedication

I dedicate *Angel Star* to my second daughter Vanessa, who graced our young family with firm will and entertaining repertoire. Her loving heart and strong faith have formed a perfect union as wife and mother. May God bless you and yours and be as a lamp unto thy feet on your journey through life.

I love you,
Dad

She is more precious than rubies,
and all the things you may desire cannot compare with her.

Proverbs 3:15

Angel Star

With scripts and skits in puppy dog tails,
  Her pleasant performance imitates.
And once in a while an ideal needs a trial,
  So sweet lady, quite ready, interrogates.

Bright and beautiful, blessed from above,
  Fine example her gender rewards.
With strong faith in truth, and trust in love,
  She leans, good and gentle things, towards.

Her story unfolds, how pretty and bold,
  Worldly gifts won of toil on this earth.
Stations yet earned awaiting her soul,
  Since the day of this Angel's blest birth.

In heaven, Sweet Lady, your crown awaits,
  But for now fragrant blooms grow here.
Until celestial home opens its gates,
  Gather arms full of flowers with cheer.

Then by and by, applause whispers low,
  Your name its melody plays.
And all the good you once made a show,
  Goes well with you all of your days.

Every Boy A Hero Narrative

I wrote this poem while assigned to a 900 person Organizational Maintenance Squadron as its second in command, Squadron Section Commander. The hours were long and days off few, preparing the coup de grace for the Soviet Empire.

In the middle of military duties, I felt my family slipping away. My son, then 11 years old, needed advice from a sometimes physically present, yet preoccupied, father. The usual quick quips, scolds and threats were dished to his impressionable young mind, but the potter's hands were missing.

We tried to bond with sports and Cub Scouting, the traditional father son activities I wanted, and practiced to some degree in my youth. I became chairman of our air-base Scout committee and managed to turn that into a bureaucratic experience instead of involvement for paternity's sake. The boy and I spent memorable times together, but they were too few. We remember well, a weekend camping trip among U.S. Civil War re-enactors that providentially tied us to a special experience years later.

During late night quiet times when he slept, I prayed and asked God to express through me His intentions for this boy. I absolutely could not have written these words without a touch of grace in my pen. Through prayer, all things are made possible and victory is often a moment away. Time is an interesting thing—anticipation lengthens its present value; pain shortens its past; and patience mollifies our doubt about future prosperity as a joy filled life lives to return it all to God.

Twelve years later, I was struck dumb and choked by emotion when my son quoted the entire verse from memory to a vanload of men at a leadership conference in Gettysburg, Pennsylvania, during our second Civil War reenactment retreat.

How did he remember it? Out of everything I said or wrote, at just the right moment in time, God threw this back at me. My boy worked hard to memorize these lines. It became an interpersonal theme for us the rest of the trip. He still shows the framed verse to anyone willing to look at it. A moment of intense joy wraps my heart like a warm spring morning, each time my son references this poem. I wrote it in difficult and uncertain times for us. It is through pure power of the Holy Spirit that he grew into a man who knows the meaning of a father's love.

We ask and God gives. We repent and He pardons. We seek and He shows His Power. We pray and He shows mercy. Some men fail but never quit; some quit before failure is apparent. All men begin life wanting to be someone's hero. God expects us to act bravely, count on His power through serene prayer, and to choose our heroes wisely.

"Against criticism a man can neither protest nor defend himself; he must act in spite of it, and then it will gradually yield to him."

Johann Wolfgang Von Goethe
(1749-1832)

German poet, novelist, scientist

Every Boy a Hero Dedication

I dedicate *Every Boy a Hero* to my son, Nicholas. He calmed our family with his supple heart and clever mind. May God bless and keep you in His loving mercy as you and yours go into the world to spread the Gospel of Christ Jesus.

I love you,
Dad

Second Dedication

I dedicate *Every Boy a Hero* to the memory of my Boy Scout Masters, the late Arthur Petersen, late Edward Evans, and Steve Brienen. To all my childhood Scout members, the wonderful people that helped me to experience joy in the great outdoors in my youth, and to all Boy Scouts of America.

In all things Be Prepared!
(In Omnia Paratus)
Jeff

And suddenly a voice came from heaven saying,
"This is my beloved <u>son</u>, in whom I am well pleased."

Matthew. 3:17

Every Boy a Hero

Every boy is a hero,
  Though not his muscle strong.
What ranks him above zero,
  Is knowing right from wrong.

When pressed by test from others,
  Courageously incline.
To tell them all your druthers,
  Let fear not voice confine.

Then with strong will you show them,
  A special lad here stands.
"Don't mess with me you pilgrim!
  I'm making noble plans."

And surely they will mock you,
  As sure as rattlers bite.
But silent others wish to,
  Be near your knightly might.

As quiet others follow,
  Their lives you save in part.
No greater glory fellow,
  Than grateful silent heart.

When through the forest slaying,
  Fierce dragons with brave sword;
For courage keep on praying,
  To Majesty our Lord.

Fear His power truly worse,
  And fight evil on strong.
Then master the universe,
  When you choose right from wrong.

Soften the Blow Narrative

"If I had known, I would rather have been a locksmith."

Albert Einstein

This is one of my earlier attempts at poetry. I first became interested in writing poetry during a freshman level creative writing class in college. I received a course grade of *C* from a professor who accused me of being, *"One of those."* It was the late 1970s and I think he was referring to me being a military veteran.

My poetry was dreadful. And needless to say, the creative writing lessons were anything but inspiring. So, I set out to pen at least one good verse on my own.

Studying and reading other poets, I began to realize the person in the verse made me want to return to his or her words. Thirty years later, I read a biography that said our second President of the United States, John Adams, told his sons, "You are never alone with a poet in your pocket."

This is more than a curious old notion. I have been comforted and intrigued many times through the arrangement of words by poets.

I wanted to discover what, *one of those* was. So, I searched through poetry to find it. Instead of finding my professor's disdain, I found myself in verses fueled by fiery pens. Be they alive or dead, male or female, I share their desire to quell loneliness as a *poet in your pocket.*

Honestly, I don't know who the little girl is in this verse. I remember picturing my daughters in my mind, but their mother would never, *scold away hurtful tears.* One of my granddaughters could easily fill in for her, but they were not born when the verse was written. My wife is the stranger in the verse, as an example justified through poetic license.

The warm tender caress of a loving mother's voice sonorously nourishes an infant's heart, gentles a child's demeanor, and resonates the essence of God's temperate rebuke; as hearts, minds, choices and actions are influenced by a sweet vibration from His female human arrangement nurturing another lovable creation—a child. These two miraculous designs of human flesh (perhaps fashioned from slow moving energy in His image), pass on God's Spirit in love.

I believe that chaos and order exist at the same time in our universe. God arranges levels of control over chaos that we recognize in our space and time as parenting, leadership and dominion—all requiring discipline in His Word to manage.

The first time I read aloud *Soften the Blow* to my sister Cindy, it made her cry. I enjoyed seeing her emotions. So, I decided to keep writing. My hope is that you take ownership of these messages and pass on the notions that bring you to a *Significant Emotional Event.*

If you find yourself laughing and crying at the same time, I call that **SEE²** or *Significant Emotional Event squared.* I'm working on a formula to describe the relationship between emotion, sound and light as it relates to heart and mind. It is, so far:

$$\text{Enlightenment} = \text{Mind} \times \textbf{SEE}^2$$

"Science arose from poetry. When times change, the two can meet again on a higher level as friends."

**Johann Wolfgang Von Goethe
(1749-1832)**

German poet, novelist, scientist

Soften the Blow Dedication

I dedicate *Soften the Blow* to my sister Cindy. You are a wonderful warm-hearted person. I never remember cutting remarks or hurtful blows. You always were my maternal figure. Thank you, Cindy, for assisting in getting me through childhood. May God bless and keep you and yours and send His Spirit to guide you home.

Love,
Jeff

*But the path of the just is like the shining sun,
that shines ever brighter unto the perfect day.*

Proverbs 4:18

Soften the Blow

As her Guardian Angel dropped his gold shield,
  Wee lass stubbed her toe, on a rock, in a field.
Good stranger came to wipe cold tears away,
  "I've called your mother, Dear. She's on her way."

Brave child's smile warmed at the stranger's caress,
  "Just look at me now, I'm a awful mess!"
Then Mother arrived with scorn on her face,
  "I've been looking for you. Why make me chase?"

No gentle voice comfort for small frame's rain,
  Nor soft kiss away the obvious pain.
Now Stranger's heart grew heavier still.
  "God, such innocence, I pray not *Your* Will."

My own little ones I cherish and hope,
  Will grow in Love's presence, able to cope.
So should another child stumble with woe,
  Someone will offer to soften the blow.

Go Easy Narrative

He who spares the rod hates his son, But he who loves him disciplines him promptly.   Proverbs 13:24

I was working as a nuclear launch officer when I penned this verse. It was influenced by a then popular movie about time travel which had the main character saying near the end, to his future parents, "If you two have a son and he burns a hole in the living room rug... go easy on him." The *go easy* stuck with me and I wrapped the poem around it.

It wasn't necessarily the theme of the movie. The *Go Easy* idea just sprang out of my need to express a belief in inter-generational behavior. I think we can pass on good and bad traits to the next generation. If we received treatment that wasn't nice or healthy, we can choose *not* to pass it on. Call it, *breaking the mold of generational behavior.*

On the other hand, the *good* needs to be perpetuated. Courteous behavior need never be out of style; nor should inappropriate young behavior go unpunished. But venting adult frustrations on children is wrong. *The Rod* is a tool of cool diligence, not a weapon of torture.

The message is simple and soft. Too often we forget simplicity is genius, while soft, is hard to do. Growing up puts the greater burden of proper behavior on the adult. But you can handle it. No matter how you were raised, break the mold if necessary and cast a new statue of courteous behavior your little ones will remember and emulate.

"The wise are instructed by reason; ordinary minds by experience; the stupid, by necessity; and brutes by instinct."

Cicero, Marcus Tullius (106 - 43 BC)
Roman author, orator, politician

Go Easy Dedication

My son was certainly in mind when I wrote this, but my dedication goes to all my high school students. Many of you received the blessings of good parenting—some did not. All of my students have the capacity to be wonderful parents. Having received a good upbringing is no guarantee of delivering a good child to society. Receiving a poor upbringing does not predestine passing it on to your children. We all must work hard and study to be good parents. In the end, if you take the time to do your homework, you will be rewarded and blessed.

Your friend and fellow life long learner,
Mr. Bair

Through wisdom a house is built,
and by understanding, it is established.

Proverbs 24:3

Go Easy

Amid life's pressure, and its maddening pace,
  A father lashed out, and slapped his son's face.
But Father of Son, remorsing this whim,
  Suffered more, when Son, went easy on him.

And when this young man grew up to a Dad,
  His son tried temper, but love struck the lad.
No remorseful whim did the pair chagrin,
  Son turned Father now, went easy again.

Then Son-of-a-son went, ambitions burning,
  Into the world, to help keep it turning.
And his Father's love inherited him,
  So when others lashed out, he went easy on them.

Nurture Narrative

I was working insanely long hours, actually entire days, weeks, and months at a time with very little rest and no family time. I've always stayed busy with life, accomplishing my next award, goal, or something. Finally, it hit me. The birth of my children and hopefully their children opened a different kind of success. Something futuristic, not short term, something bigger had to be considered.

Nurture was written while I was in the Air Rescue Service. My children were 15, 12, and 11 years old. I was pressured to invest in an expensive California home by well meaning associates, but I refused their advice. Looking at the military families around us, I began to realize I could lose something more precious than my next promotion. I heard my unborn grandchildren calling to me in a nondescript pattern. Ambition for personal recognition gave way to enjoying the company of my children and wife. Dialogue with older airmen unwrapped a certainty in my brain. They were convincing me of the fickle nature of personal glory versus fealty of family. Prosperity begins at home. Success in home-life takes practice.

I volunteered for an assignment to a place my heart told me my family and I could enjoy and come together upon a new reliance in each others company. Becky and I said our prayers and when the orders came through, we realized it would eventually begin the end of our military life. My early promotion would not materialize after all. The strangeness of change came on quickly. Yet small pieces of personal glory clung to my nature like epoxy, causing great pain each time a vestige tore from its well-cured grip.

This was very difficult to experience. Clinging to a decaying system after it was obviously over, now seems so terribly petty. Yet, at the time, it was all I knew and wanted.

So, we returned to rural southwest Germany (unified East and West) for two years, and I found my family waiting there for me with open arms. We all discovered more about ourselves among the pleasant diversions Europe offers.

When I closed my eyes for a restful sleep in that fairy tale place of castles, maidens and jousting knights, I could hear small voices and see my grandchildren, whom I almost missed. Our futures are made by the very nature of our choices and actions taken. Through freedom of choice we succeed if God's counsel is first relied upon. Choice by our own design has as its indemnity, forgiveness, if we recognize God's glory and trust in the Name of His Son Jesus *The Christ.*

How much fuller is a life that understands forgiveness, yet makes choices only after prayer with the ruler of space and time. Prove it to yourself today. Pray before your next decision, and mark the arrival of right-things as God answers faithfully.

"I must study politics and war that my sons may have liberty to study mathematics and philosophy. My sons ought to study mathematics and philosophy, geography, natural history, naval architecture, navigation, commerce and agriculture in order to give their children a right to study painting, poetry, music, architecture, statuary, tapestry, and porcelain."

John Adams
(1735-1826)

Second President
First Vice President
Of the United States of America

Nurture Dedication

I dedicate *Nurture* to my Foster Sister Karen Gaines. You were always a good example of nurturing behavior. I looked to your parenting model as inspiration for raising my own children. As a caring, concerned person, you continue to inspire strong will in moral judgment and good sense in friendly spirit.

With brotherly love,
Jeff

Second Dedication

I dedicate *Nurture* to my grandchildren. You visited my mind and touched my heart with your spirits even before you were born. How much more wonderful and blessed are we for you being with us? May the God of our universe shed His eternal blessings upon you like cool sweet water in a dry place.

I love you,
Grandpa Bair

Children's children are the crown of old men,
and the glory of children is their father.

Proverbs 17:6

Nurture

Wow! I nearly missed you,
  Your gentle smiling face.
The way you coo when tummy full,
  And diaper dry in place.

Near missed your soft cheek kisses,
  Ruddy little toothless grin.
Giddy bellicose babble,
  Wet slobber down small chin.

Forsook the day I met you,
  Now rue the day you leave.
I almost missed you sweetie,
  And all that you achieve.

God has other plans for us,
  You me, His faithful heirs.
Starting down a road well lit,
  I fell down prideful stairs.

 In my stumbling manner,
  A narrow path did guide;
Toward a homespun clavichord,
  To sing your birth beside.

The past but a moment gone,
  Our present fleeting fast.
You're here to God's love endow,
  True pride of me at last.

Love Everlasting Narrative

This poem took years to clean up. The middle stanzas wrote themselves first. The beginning was the tough part. The ending two stanzas flowed easily off my pen.

Poems like this one are labors of conscience. There was an unseen presence requiring its completion. You must understand that poetry flows from a stream of consciousness influenced by unseen forces. As gravity pulls at water flowing in a brook to make it bubble resonantly, something draws poetry out of us. It is as a liquid that sometimes is viscous and runs smoothly, yet more often coagulates under a cold callous perception of mortal concern. Only a free spirit can tap into the sugary nectar of words that flow easily like maple sap, condensed into a sweeter, thicker mixture of colorful context to nourish and quiet a soul.

This verse began as a notion about good girls gone bad. My heart sinks at the thought or sight of a young woman who forgets her virtues. Women are so beautiful and powerful when they follow God's laws and live in regard of His principles. I suppose they feel the same about men.

The message is clear. As Jesus bravely rescued a woman accused of adultery from stoning, then rebuked her, "Go and sin no more." (John 8: 2-11), the spirit yearns for all women to follow the narrow path that leads to a fruitful life—an existence that makes and nurtures the image of God!

Stand behind Jesus as he draws a line in the sands of time to separate you from evil. Accept His guidance, protection and rebuke. Learn about the lie of keeping yourself in a high state of esteem over others (including your family) ridiculing sacrifice. Choose to submit to the life God intends for you. Then find real peace, great happiness, fulfillment and joy, as you live for another person's contentment.

Reprove the evil spirit and repent of your sins through Jesus Christ and watch the nay-sayers and threats to your joy slink away as the mob left the adulteress (John 8: 1-11) unharmed and protected by the power of God. Above all, when the clouds of doubt subside as you follow a new path towards living a *Joy Filled Life*, lay each burden down and thank God for His love, mercy and faithfulness.

Please remember to give God the glory for your blessings. If you stumble, ask Him again for forgiveness and rise up renewed. Keep to the narrow path, which is lit to see only one footstep at a time. Soon you will come to a modest gate and there Jesus will lead you into the light and you will see much further.

"I am more and more convinced that Man is a dangerous creature, and that power whether vested in many or a few is ever grasping, and like the grave cries give, give. The great fish swallow up the small, and he who is most strenuous for the Rights of the people, when vested with power, is as eager after the prerogatives of Government. You tell me of degrees of perfection to which Humane Nature is capable of arriving, and I believe it, but at the same time lament that our admiration should arise from the scarcity of the instances."

**Abigail Adams
(1744-1818)**

First Lady
of the United States of America

Love Everlasting Dedication

I dedicate *Love Everlasting* to all good-girls gone bad. As was the case with the adulteress, once forgiven you can return to a fruitful life. With God's glory as your reason for living, He will give you the desires of your heart. Accept His rebuke and then, *go and sin no more.* You came into the world flawed yet beautiful. Through Jesus Christ you can ask God to forgive your unwise choices in life, forgive yourself and ask others to forgive you if necessary. Once you are free of sin, do not return to the life style that blinded you from truth and joy.

Your friend,
Jeff

*Who can say, "I have made my heart clean,
I am pure from my sin?"*

Proverbs 20:9

Love Everlasting

Once there was a child, who knew she always could,
  . Dominating people held, that she never would.
With legs straight and sturdy, her eyes searching up,
  Innocence became her, like a newborn pup.

As bright eyed child grew, up to be a maiden,
  Folks stared and cursed her, lamp lit treasures laden.
Strong will was led by faith, in a living God,
  No scorn dissuaded, her feminine resolve.

Then came the force of evil,
  Temptation did abide.
Grown woman once a lady,
  Began to cheat and lie.

As darkness overshadowed,
  Her light at once went out.
Remorseful heart was stricken,
  And cried a prayerful shout.

The Angels heard her crying,
  And humbled her to God.
A beautiful white stallion,
  Was harnessed, combed, and shod.

Away the steed did carry,
  Sweet lady's grief and fears.
Until her light rekindled,
  And dried regretful tears.

With strength renewed she awoke,
  And asked her precious Lord,
"Why came You when forsaken,
  I left You for the horde?"

Remember when you struggled, for faith in Me abide,
Repentance brought your light back, the same as when I died.

And so this lovely lady dwells, within a hallowed peace,
  Her wonder never over, that troubles never cease.
Yet in her darkest hour, when all seems laid to waste,
  His Cross reminds her often, A Love Forever Chaste.

My Things Narrative

All families seem to experience the borrowing curse. Someone's stuff is taken and the alarm from its lawful owner sounds an indignant blare of righteous restitution owed. Most infractions of family borrowing are minor infringements on personal space or possessions. The answer to calming these annoying noises can be simple, yet difficult to accomplish.

When I attended the United States Air Force Officer Training School at Lackland Air Force Base, San Antonio, Texas in the summer of 1984, a lesson was taught that helped greatly. We had an honor code that stated, "I will not lie, cheat, steal or tolerate anyone who does." To help keep our pledge and honor, we instituted in our small group, a promise to one-another, "Anything I have is yours for using, and you don't need to ask me before borrowing."

We meant what we said too. I lived, worked and studied with honorable men and women. We shared most everything and achieved great goals. However, the one thing that seemed to matter most, was our giving to each other the credit for all our accomplishments.

Three months spent in OTS were the finest days of my professional military experience. Our word was our bond. Never before, nor after, have I shared such unselfish, honorable company packed with team building and individual accomplishments. How I long for a never-ending repeat of this type of worthy existence among professionals—sacrifice and accomplishment blended to perfection.

Our founding fathers modeled it for us when they signed the most pivotal document in creating this unique nation we call home—The Declaration of Independence. **"And for the support of this Declaration with a firm reliance on the protection of divine providence, we mutually pledge to each other our lives, our fortunes, and our sacred honor."**

It is not to be confused with socialism, villages or communism. The American motive for earning and sharing comes from the innate wisdom in liberty of conscience, stewardship of prosperity and freedom to choose charitableness. All other models for redistributing property, intellectual or otherwise, fail in their execution. Incentive, charity and choice are best.

This concept, I passed on to my children and today as adults, they all share and give without hesitation. It is a proud sight to see my family continue this tradition and pass onto their children honor in selflessness that once made my heart soar like a hawk.

We can and must, expect the best behavior and treatment from each other. There is plenty of scriptural reference to reinforce God's laws requiring an excellent approach to being principled and expecting respect and trust from one another.

I believe we should be professional grandparents, parents, siblings, sons and daughters. We can be excellent to one another and still relax in each other's company. Familiarity in a disciplined family will not breed contempt while God's love is nurtured!

So, be first-rate to each other. Unyoke the burden of disquiet around family familiarity. Tolerate none of God's laws broken, but treat each other as you would be treated and allow the family to always exist in harmony with learning from mistakes through God's second most precious gift (after choice), forgiveness. Then your children will come home to visit along with their children, and all will relish the shared event until God's blessings bring you close again, safe, joyful and full of the Holy Spirit—in awe of great prosperity and wealth in family ties.

"To err is human; to forgive, divine."
Alexander Pope
(1688-1744)
English Poet

My Things Dedication

I dedicate *My Things* to my family and their children to pass on as a reminder to respect others property and to pledge not to lie, cheat, steal or tolerate anyone who does. May God's commandments become your banner to rally around when temptation comes knocking. Also, may His blessing of wisdom require you to be vigilant of thieves but generous to honorable people.

Always with you,
Father

He who has a bountiful eye will be blessed.
For he gives of his bread to the poor.

Proverbs 22:8

My Things

Someone took my hairbrush!
  And someone took my comb.
Why can't they all just leave,
  My private things alone!

Simple for a just man,
  He bothers others' not.
My gimbal brained family,
  Just takes what's not their lot.

I try to mind my manners,
  Why can't they practice theirs?
My property is mine so,
  I can pass it to my heirs!

My children won't wish for,
  Possessions not their own.
As I freely share mine,
  Until the day they're grown.

As we understand that,
  All things belong to Him.
Deeds borrowed for awhile,
  Pass love on to our kin.

'Til the race is over,
  What's mine is yours 'til then.
For what is ours is His,
  As He takes 'way our sin.

And what things recon more,
  Desirable than trust.
The King asks only faith,
  For His Love, honor must.

Old Porch Door Narrative

This poem was an early attempt at communicating a lesson or two from an actual experience. At age 13, I was riding my bicycle (a golden metal flake, 5 gear Huffy Stingray) to church. I got up good speed on a downhill street and at the bottom of the asphalt road where some gravel had accumulated, I hit the hand brakes too hard, skidded, and wiped out.

Like an angel out of nowhere, a man picked me up and took me into his house where his wife administered first-aid. Looking back over 36 years ago, I can't recall their faces or much detail around the incident, but I vividly remember their actions and kindness.

The pain is gone. A scar remains. Yet, in dream like clarity their perfect behavior quickens my pulse. When I focus on the incident, my palms sweat and nerves tense in preparation for the tumble. It's a kind of uncomfortable exhilaration remembering the panic. It is punishment and curious blessings at the same time.

We are vulnerable and resilient at once. Accidents are like warnings against stretching too far into the unknown. It's the edge of physical harm we sometimes seek in order to excel in the flesh. Pushing the edge of any envelope in God's earthly realm subjects us to losing touch with His laws and principles.

Eventually, tragedy prevails and we shake our heads in wonderment over bad luck, poor choice, a curse or some other rationalized excuse. A sort of intoxication consumes our better judgment. Through pain, we are brought back to the reality of physical limitations, but not before we idolize the thrill.

Throughout my life, more strangers have shared kindness with me during other trials. I have been mentored, rebuked, bandaged and encouraged by loving people who had no stake in the outcome. I know now that each of them was one of God's agents of mercy.

My prayer today is that I can share God's love often enough to please Him, the way that old man and woman lifted me up and lightened my burden.

The boy's bike is a different color and he is younger to help with meter in the verse, but the rest was me and very real. I know their gift continues to dry tears and soothe wounds today. Please help pass on their message and God will bless you too.

"My opinion is that in the world of knowledge the idea of *good* appears last of all, and is seen only with an effort; and, when seen, is also inferred to be the universal author of all things beautiful and right, parent of light in this visible world, and immediate source of reason and truth in the intellectual; and that this is the power upon which he who would act rationally, either in public or private life must have his eye fixed."

Plato
(427 — 347 BC)

Greek philosopher
Student of Socrates, Teacher of Aristotle

Old Porch Door Dedication

I dedicate *Old Porch Door* to my brother John. He made it to church that day ahead of me. As I was learning God's message of *love thy neighbor* first hand through the kindness of strangers, John was receiving God's message at church. May God bless your life with peace and joy.

Love,
Jeff

Do not withhold good from those to whom it is due,
when it is in the power of your hand to do so.

Proverbs 3:27

Old Porch Door

Nine years old, with few summer days to last,
  Legs spurred red bike, down a gravel slick road.
Marbles on glass met a bald tire fast,
  As off spilled a clumsy bodily load.

Sharp burning pain was as instantly felt,
  As the old man who appeared by young side.
On creaky bent knee, worn bones careful knelt,
  Gracious voice calming, lone pitiful tide.

Blistered white paint, on rickety shorn boards,
  Scattered out of the way, workaday boots.
Hinges dry rusted, on squeaky screen door,
  Caved way to great arms, protecting their loot.

Kind wife met them there, with bandage and salve,
  Her soft caring manner, transcending time.
Rich kitchen aromas, numbed painful calf,
  Bloody flesh, full of road gravel and grime.

Mem'ry fades faces, but what matters more,
  Their spontaneous love now referencing.
A stranger carried through that old porch door,
  Portrays God, and man circumferencing.

So immortal are they, for kindness shared,
  As one passes on to others their gift.
Be not afraid to depart this old world,
  If over a threshold, someone's burden, you once lift.

Part 2

This anthology of prose, poetry and proverbs is a collection of verse by engraved theme. It seems we must experience ridiculous in order to enjoy the sublime.

Now into most every life a little rain must fall, darkness shadow, or sin shake down courage like wintry wind blows through a dark night to chill and numb senses. And sometimes, it's worse.

Please bear with the next few verses. They were written at times of want for personal reconciliation with our Creator, self-rebuke, and introspection. There are hours and years of work here, and what seems simple is, or was, terribly complex. Obvious failure is often obscured from our vision until we take a moment to reflect. The reflection is seldom pretty, but a new image can be made beautiful with time, practice and grace.

We are given a great gift at birth—choice. How we choose to live our lives makes all the difference. This next section describes choices made and their outcomes. As you read ask yourself, "What choices would I make?" Then read on into *Part 3* to find out what preference I chose.

"Why read poetry?" you ask, because of *Fire, Focus* and *Finish*.

As spontaneous combustion starts a blaze, the poet burns. As a solitary star captures the heart and imagination of an astronomer, the poet concentrates. And as the architect lives to see his plans take shape, I labored to build an expression in which resides the soft salient existence of meaningful moments lived, dreams shared and hope restored.

Read on, reflect often and choose wisely. For our choices often accustom less than happiness and fall short of any possibility for joy, unless God is first relied upon to host their discernment. Uninspired choices will always miss the target center of great opportunity. Hidden from our view is the full measure of how grand the victory could have been, because our Creator is merciful and does not want us to suffer a loss from a challenge we did not try to embrace.

Yet mediocrity punishes (with regret) those who never risk earthly tones to reach triumphant harmony. The lament of worthy deeds *undone* tolls like a death knell gonging slowly, methodically, choking its victim with putrid rhetoric that never ceases. Those, close by, either heap invective on the suffering miscreant or wallow with him; loving misery more than joy. Trusting in the LORD is risky. Its rewards are as clear as forced rhyme and as prescient as allegorical rhythm.

"Far better to dare mighty things, to win glorious triumphs, even though checkered by failure, than to take rank with those poor spirits who neither enjoy much nor suffer much, because they live in the gray twilight that knows not victory, nor defeat."

Theodore Roosevelt
(1858-1919)

26th President
of the United States of America

Part 2 Dedication

I dedicate this section to my brother Steven. You were in my thoughts and prayers during reflection as I prepared to express my experiences in poetry. How much more Joyful are we having come through the fire, accepting God's love for us. May God bless and nourish your faith, "...so that your place will never be with those cold and timid souls who know neither victory nor defeat."

Love,
Jeff

*Trust in the Lord with all your heart,
and lean not on your own understanding.*

Proverbs 3:5

El Toro Narrative

I desire to speak Spanish but alas, my brain cells do not align easily for foreign language comprehension. A weak constitution for indulgences disavows my effort to force it, as well. Enjoying a Spanish holiday in 1977, I witnessed several bullfights one afternoon. During the battles I realized sometimes the crowd cheers the matador and sometimes they cheer the bull. Yet, the bull always dies in the end. In one fight, the bull rose back up after being pierced by what the matador thought was the final blow from his sword, and gored the unsuspecting athlete between his legs. I actually have this on super 8 film!

The crowd went nuts waving white cloths and cheering the bull, but in the end, the bull still died. That was an afternoon indelible; one day in my life, 30 years ago, and I remember it like it was yesterday. What happens when a metaphor becomes reality? How will we handle the torment? How long will it last, and by what energy or power will we endure?

"...It is not the critic who counts: not the man who points out how the strong man stumbles or where the doer of deeds could have done better. The credit belongs to the man who is actually in the arena, whose face is marred by dust and sweat and blood, who strives valiantly, who errs and comes up short again and again, because there is no effort without error or shortcoming, but who knows the great enthusiasms, the great devotions, who spends himself for a worthy cause; who, at best, knows, in the end, the triumph of high achievement, and who, at the worst, if he fails, at least he fails while daring greatly, so that his place shall never be with those cold and timid souls who knew neither victory nor defeat."

Theodore Roosevelt,
(1858-1919)
26th President of the United States of America
"Citizenship in a Republic" Speech at the Sorbonne, Paris, April 23, 1910

El Toro Dedication

I dedicate *El Toro* to the bull in all of us. We enjoy or seek green pastures of leisure and pleasure only to eventually find ourselves in the arena. May God Bless each one of us as we offer our lives up to His power, glory and grace to be made to lie down in green pastures like a lamb and avoid the Matador's final blow.

To the Bull,
Jeff

*How much better it is to get wisdom than gold!
And to get understanding is to be chosen rather than silver.*

Proverbs 16:16

El Toro

By and by, I could rely an
  Enemy's sword would hilt,
Deep in my breast, Oh! heaviness,
  Release the craven guilt.

I pray only for, Matador,
  Your keen steel blade, heart finds.
For Picador, hath pricked before,
  Blood trickles down fine lines.

At shaft length rode terse Toreador,
  His blunt point pierced not deep.
And now I find my heart and mind,
  Numb, and weary for sleep.

One final blow, so soul will know,
  The rest it likens for.
Then from this earth, sins finally pass,
  Through eternity's glad door.

Ode to Mortal Soul Narrative

After watching and studying another movie rendition of Shakespeare's Hamlet, I tried to write a brief explanation of his soliloquy for my own reflection. It proved very difficult. How could something as simple as, "...to be or not to be?" be so complex? Is it a question, or is it a statement? Sages on human thinking have probably considered this notion ever since Shakespeare wrote it centuries before our college, or high school, literature classes dealt with it.

I don't want to rehash intellectual property here or wax on like sociology, or psychology professors. Yet, six English words confound. Most people get to a point in their lives and finally confront their mortality asking, "Why am I here?"

The following verse is an attempt to discern meaning from this famous script. It truly was just for me to concentrate on for awhile. Then, like all simple subjects, it got complicated. Before long, I put it away.

I almost quit on this one. But it kept poking me when I brushed by it in my other work. And of course, I had not answered Mr. Shakespeare's question. So, I stopped trying to solve the Hamlet Riddle and asked God in prayer. He made it simple for me. God has a way of doing that you know.

"The soul's safety is in its heat. Truth without enthusiasm, morality without emotion, ritual without soul, makes for a Church without power. Destitute of the fire of God, nothing else counts; possessing Fire, nothing else matters.

Samuel Chadwick
(1840-1932)

English Methodist Theologian, Spiritualist

Ode to Mortal Soul Dedication

I dedicate *Ode to Mortal Soul* to my brother Mike. You are a kind reminder of pleasant youthful things, and of "Dad's wavy black hair." May God bless you with the understanding of all things difficult made simple through His grace.

Love,
Jeff

*In all your ways acknowledge Him,
and he shall direct your paths.*

Proverbs 3:6

Ode to Mortal Soul (On Hamlet's Soliloquy)

Having lived a bit, I understand,
How he languished, over the anguish to
Describe utter contempt for misfortune.
Even deeper ran, scribed by pen and hand,
A need to paint pain, and turmoil inside;
Inherent, it troubles every man's brain.

He speaks for us a rhetorical quiz:
What right or reasons have we, *"to be?"*
None better sells this curiosity than mortality.
A merger with unfortunate trials of
Hurt, fear, grief, abandonment; therein lies the matter.
By ourselves suffering, what together, we ought not.

Yet it seems we collectively are doomed,
To repeat thousands of years of mistakes;
Unless a greater cause captures awareness.
Then the great shapers of mass appeal,
Endure as fragile a resistance to
Self destruction, as the individual.

Without an answer, *"to be or not..."*
Endangering the very essence
Of collective reasoning enmasse;
Doomed to topple the best conceived unions of man.

In Hamlet lies a reckoning, but no answer.
For if the King falls what becomes of Denmark?
Of this dilemma solace remains in the hands
Of his Creator—faith alone restores hope.

And hope should be greater than reasoning.
While man shrinks from action,
A tortured soul remains alive.
Living requires a Miracle—I call mine Love.

I Too a Fool Narrative

This is an old one. It rhymed rather quickly and except for tinkering with it over the years, it was pretty well finished after the first draft. *I Too a Fool* was inspired by reading the Bible and a very lovely poem by Edward R. Sill (April 29, 1841–February 27, 1887), "The Fools Prayer."

I learned a little late in life that it's okay to suggest oneself a fool, but not to call someone else a fool—even though they may be one. Another one of those simple conundrums you ask? Well, yes it is. Suffice to say, it really is to one's advantage to be released from the burden of judging others and concentrate on judging only one's self. Here we tread on insecure ground, as we stray from trust in God's plans, to worry about our own. It's another faithful, simple choice we can make. But, wow! It is difficult to do.

This is an early attempt at self-deprecating verse to help ameliorate pent up pride, and I've been practicing ever since. I seem to be in as much trouble today judging others as I was 20 years ago when I wrote this poem. I pray for forgiveness, ask people wronged for their pardon and just keep judging them. This one will take awhile, but I'm determined to beat it—with God's help.

"Take note, theologians, that in your desire to make matters of faith out of propositions relating to the fixity of the sun and earth, you run the risk of eventually having to condemn as heretics those who would declare the earth to stand still and the sun to change position; eventually, I say, at such a time as it might be proved that the earth moves and the sun stands still."

Galileo Galilei
(1564-1642)
Italian physicist and astronomer

I Too A Fool Dedication

I dedicate *I Too A Fool* to my own sinful ways. May I continue to reflect on the fool's loss and battle judging others until God's mercy for my sin is no longer required. Then I can pass this verse on to someone else to own.

Jeff

Better is the poor who walks in his integrity,
than one who is perverse in his lips and is a fool.

Proverbs 19:1

I Too A Fool

He bristled at a lark then,
  One bright red sunshine darkened.
Mere chance his only tool,
  Young man, I too a fool.

Bright eyes too early blackened,
  By drunken springtime slackened.
Forbidden fruit partook,
  Until his courage shook.

Sweet sticky juices flowing,
  Down lips from words all knowing.
Dove's white whispering wings,
  Raised chills, while Sirens sing.

Did not nourish Wisdom's gruel,
  Bland to taste for you poor fool.
Lick the bowl while you may,
  Or belch regret one day.

No chance bet this cup of mead,
  Summer spell spent fear and greed.
Few choose the path less used,
  Like you, I too a fool.

The Toast Narrative

One of the many things I learned on active duty was how to drink. As an enlisted person, it was just a few beers at football parties and other sporting events. I didn't keep much alcohol in my home, but on bowling nights I put a few away with the guys. My first break in active duty service had me in the Air National Guard. There, we partied every chance we got. The camaraderie was intense and it felt like the fraternity I never got to experience in college. Yet, it never got out of hand.

By the time I went to Officer Training School, I knew how to handle myself at drinking events. One of our favorite watering holes, the OTSOM (Officer Training School Open Mess), was a raucous joint filled with bygone memorabilia of aeronautical feats and the mystique of professional social engagement.

We worked, studied and exercised hard for weeks until we earned the privilege to patronize the club bar. I'll always remember the fellowship and fun of unwinding with my fellow Officer Trainees. We drank moderately, aware of the negative effects of drunkenness.

But the drinking really got going at Missile Officer parties. I didn't have any clinical trouble with alcohol, but there were some late nights when I closed down the Officer's Club lounge, drinking beer and talking with our favorite Colonel. In my time-off, while helping on a local half-mile racetrack pit crew, partying was prevalent and well controlled.

Shortly before missile duty was over, I quit drinking all together. I was counseling subordinates for DWI, DUI and imposing disciplinary actions for inappropriate drunken behavior. So I decided to set a better example by not drinking. I took up a soda water with lime and socialized accordingly. During my last active duty assignment in Germany, I found a delightful nonalcoholic beer to my liking.

Of course a word of warning is required here. Alcohol is a mood altering drug. It can cause liver or kidney damage, birth defects and other physical harm if abused, ingested by people of low tolerance, or mixed with other drugs. Alcohol is deadly if consumed too quickly over a short period of time. Every year, unbridled drinking binges kill college students, G.I.s and others who should never have started drinking because their motives were wrong to begin with.

Also, an eternal vigil needs to be directed towards the elimination of drinking while driving and under-age drinking. Some progress has been made towards abatement of drunk driving, and youth drinking. Yet, until we can assure ourselves that no one is intoxicated behind the wheel of any vehicle, our public concern for drinking and driving should stay on high alert. Our attention to lessening children's exposure to alcohol should not be lost or relaxed. Finally, booze and any dangerous activity like boating, swimming, skiing, handling equipment, etcetera, should be strictly curtailed for public and private safety.

We don't need another constitutional amendment to penalize the whole of society because a few over indulgers can't control their behavior. What we aught to do, is use the consumption of alcoholic beverages as a moderate behavior with a firm commitment to treating it as a legal drug. In that frame of reference, it becomes a substance to use without abuse and avoid if we don't need it, want it or can't handle it.

One last word of caution. Insidious people will use drinking as an opportunity to influence your behavior, take advantage of your body, or hold you hostage to its effects. Do not put yourself into any uncomfortable situation trying to defend an alcohol related incident. Just avoid the parties and drinking events to insure peace of mind by eliminating an alcohol hang-over that could last a life time.

I now consume alcoholic beverages in moderation and prescribe to the healthy effects of it. I proved to myself there are no addictions with God's help! Chemical dependencies are avoided or won over through proper choices and self-discipline. Lacking this resolve, don't drink!

If you need help in the battle against exposing your mind and body to the unhealthy effects of alcohol or any mood altering drug, get on with it! *None of us is as smart as all of us.*

Also, no one person has all the strength needed to fight and win against temptations and chemical dependencies. Start with a prayer and a humble heart. Ask God right now to help you get over the problems that cause your bad choices to persist. He will not be available until you trust and follow His rules, and as my favorite Gospel music artist Jerry Wise sings, "...when you abide in Him, He will abide in you."

You'll know when you have truly found God, because all your trepidation, beyond the healthy fear of Him, fades and addictions you once thought you had, are realized as excuses for chosen behavior.

"To be always intending to live a new life, but never find time to set about it, is as if a man should put off eating and drinking from one day to another till he be starved and destroyed."

**Sir Walter Scott
(1771-1832)**

Scottish author, novelist

The Toast Dedication

I dedicate *The Toast* to my OTS comrades, and Uncle Eddy. May you find a comfortable place to unwind and in moderation imbibe with friends.

Your friend,
Jeff

Have you found Honey?
Eat only as much as you need,
lest you be filled with it and vomit.

Proverbs 25:16

The Toast

Imbibe in our libation they say,
   And drink the fruit of the vine.
We won't get fed, until you partake,
   Lacking quaff, we cannot dine.

Imbibe in our libation they croon,
   The night is turning out drab.
When we libate, the fun starts quite soon,
   Have a drink, you *Big Old Crab!*

Imbibe, Imbibe, Imbibe! the crowd burst,
   Then off we will shove, Old Mate.
Not doused the first? Oh, terrible thirst!
   Please hurry! Catch up! Too late.

"Imbribe in our liblashion," they slur,
   Then you too can be as cool.
It's not over, our unguided tour,
   Look! There's Babbs with her head in the stool.

Enough! Enough! I will not imbibe,
   You give good reason to quit.
Punch drunk as a barbarian tribe,
   Forgot the occasion? Libation took over it.

Candle Lament Narrative

From January through October 1990, I spent ten wonderful months in the Air Rescue Service as Executive to the Commander. I traveled extensively to Alaska, and visited Japan, Okinawa, Korea, the North Central United States, Florida, Illinois and Mississippi. I was planning the commander's next trip to a new location when he decided to return to Alaska (the Colonel loved going there).

We arrived by civilian air carrier and made our way to the airbase near Anchorage. I remember going for a quick run in the dim early evening sunlight that cast ghostly grey shadows and seeing a moose nibbling on a small tree. As I arrived at my colonel's suite to begin the trip to our evening meal with many of his Air Rescue subordinates, a melancholy scene unfolded before me.

The commander opened his door while speaking to someone on the phone. He motioned me to enter, and I sat down in an overstuffed chair across from him trying not to listen in on his conversation. I couldn't help but notice his countenance change from cordial and familiar to sullen and grieved.

He was a young man. He had health, strength, agility and a kind heart. He treated me like a son with wise counsel, and included me in important matters. He asked my opinion on lofty subjects, and gave me increased responsibilities over difficult tasks. He introduced me to senators and statesmen, generals and dignitaries. I loved him as a friend, and respected his adventurous ways tempered by awareness in strength of influence and power of position. So when he rested the phone on its cradle and looked at me, I was deeply saddened by the tears in his eyes.

The Air Force had just told him he would not receive the rank of General and he said the reason was, timing. He had been serving in a brigadier general's job as a full colonel with the understanding that when congress approved funding for an impending number of general slots, he would surely be one of the recipients. What no one was counting on was the rapid implosion of the Soviet Empire as well as the even more rapid drawing down of our military strength.

Over the next few years, entire wings, bases, and special units evaporated at the stroke of legislative pens. Tens of thousands of G.I. lives changed forever. The very essence of our beings seemed dashed upon cold hard rocks by waves of *draw-downs.*

It all came into focus for the two of us that night in the quaintly furnished receiving room of his private DV suite. He would be gone from active duty within a few weeks and I lingered for a couple more years, but his tears sealed the deal. It was real now. The military didn't need our services anymore and was permanently laying us off.

That night, we went on to a nice seafood restaurant dinner shared with a dozen or so of our loyal comrades and their wives. He would not broach the subject with other subordinates until we returned to headquarters and made arrangements for handing off the reigns-of-command.

Later, the Colonel began telling me his retirement plans as he hurried to finish some last minute projects and began to pass the mantle of responsibility onto the next commander.

The new commander made changes, and I was one of them. I moved my office to base headquarters and received my own command of over 400 base support people. This was a good time. It provided a beginning transition for my family and me.

Candle Lament was written on a C-130 transport airplane on a trip to Pacific Rim countries, visiting units my Colonel owned. The murmur of propeller engines hummed in my ears and resonated through my body, as we crossed the ocean for too many hours to count. I sat in a web sling seat most of the trip while the *drone, drone, drone* of airplane engines caused me to slip easily into a poetic state of mind.

As light passes through window glass or heat through a solid cold surface, I believe these words passed through me to my pen. I had to write them down. The reason *Candle Lament* is on paper is that I followed my poet-warrior heart. Like a moth drawn to a flame or a bat to its echo, some nascent energy drove my hand until pen strokes coalesced in a descriptive pattern on paper for later digestion.

Was it written to express my Colonel's tears, or my own fears? Was it written for the thousands of accomplished aviators and their families suffering the demise of their industry, their livelihoods, their safe harbor, their beloved wing, squadron, or Air Force? I don't know. You read and decide.

For once on a long journey sailing over an ocean of unending waves, a young man entranced by the harmony of an airman's heartbeat, absorbed his physical surroundings. Influenced by the times, molded by the past, and intrigued by the future, he wrote a poem lamenting the irony of a job well done receiving as its final reward, the opportunity to start all over again, in a different life.

"The Story is told that one night at dinner here at Mount Vernon; Lafayette said to Washington, 'General, you Americans even in war and desperate times have a superb spirit. You're happy and you're confident. Why is it?' And Washington answered, 'There is freedom. There is space for a man to be alone and think, and there are friends who owe each other nothing but affection.'"

Ronald Reagan
(1911-2004)
40th President of the United States of America

250th anniversary of George Washington's birth
Mount Vernon, Virginia, February 22, 1982

Candle Lament Dedication

I dedicate *Candle Lament* to my Colonel, his beloved late Air Rescue and Air Weather Services, Pararescue men, Hurricane Hunters, pilots, special forces, maintenance troops, and all their support comrades and the mission. May God bless and keep you and yours safe for the service you gave "That Others May Live."

Your servant,
Captain J. L. Bair

*The lot is cast into the lap,
but its every decision is from the Lord.*

Proverbs 16:33

Candle Lament

Woe, woe, woe,
Moves like a candles flow,
Under blue and yellow glow,
Teardrops of paraffin know,
How tragedy strikes, then goes.
Solidifies clinging to cold hard glass,
Next to, not holding fast.
Easily peeled off then,
Teardrops begin again.
This time drip rate slow,
Under blue and yellow glow.
Gravity pulling past,
Eyelids of cold hard glass,
Settling layers deep,
Oh! how the Reaper gleans his keep.
Pooling deep paraffin pooling steep,
Surely you'll overflow the heap.
Magnificent warm cool mass,
Clinging to cold hard glass.
Motion and timing right
Flickering in the night.
Until at wicks end,
Flame no longer can transcend.
Whiff of burnt wax lingers on.
Spirit of smoke rises beyond.
Hearts filled with wonder at the sight,
Darkness' images in the night.
Then once focused, there is new light.

Paradox Narrative

"Yet hope remains, while the company is true."
J.R.R. Tolkien, Lord of the Rings

When I was a freshman in high school in 1971, I was walking home one cool autumn evening and I began to talk to God. I have spoken directly to our Creator for as long as I can remember, but in my youth, I failed to recognize His replies.

God's subtle way of answering my prayers slipped past an unskilled mind. My senses were dull to the benefits of child like faith, as I practiced overly liberal, secular, humanistic behavior—a product of misguided youth. I found myself rejecting the Spirit for all kinds of selfish reasons. The search was on for truth in idealistic, mature adventures, without relying on the faith of a child to support the journey. Still, every now and then, the kid would pinch my consciousness and beg for clarity of purpose.

As years passed, I vividly recalled this autumn prayer I made at an age between childhood and maturing adult. It was a huge request at the time, and was a test to see if God was really listening. I wanted to believe the notions and stories told by professional religious teachers and supported by doltish adults. At this point, I hadn't read much of the Bible. I had various interpretations of *The Word* read to me and discussed in catechism, but I had not searched it out for myself. This was a time of immature foolishness.

I've had an interest in history and world affairs most of my life. So on that cool, fragrant, Fall evening, as I slogged through small piles of crunchy leaves on my way home from a late school event, I asked God to *take down the Berlin Wall.* While the world was captivated by it, I was concerned for the millions of people held captive behind it. What seems unimportant or nostalgic now, was then horrifyingly real and considered a common threat to our security. Great men and women mentioned it in context with overwhelming troubles, trials and lofty geo-political conundrums yearning for caution.

Driven by fear, these issues smoldered behind smaller vestiges of tinder dry conflicts that unnervingly prodded at our lives, robbing our hearts of happiness and slowly destroying our national will to support and defend the Constitution. The fear gripped our nation so tightly that it still drives some prominent Americans (educated in the season of that reality), with *any*-war hatred and social order imperative—to a fault.

I grew up learning from school, first hand accounts, and the media, about WWII, Korea, Vietnam, communism and the Cold War. These were powerful issues then. They were real, yet terribly confusing at the time. How eagerly we want to forget these things, which once defined our dysfunctional national character, giving birth to hardened beliefs of yet another human design for a civilization without hope, lacking virtue, embracing common culture as truth. Thus, we nearly aborted the birth of our divinely ordained and spiritually kept, fragile independence.

My concern was for the people denied freedom. Even though we didn't talk about it much, the Cold War was constantly in the back of our minds. A news break or headline would jerk our collective consciousness back to the subject we tried to bury in everyday work, school and play. It steeped our culture in fear and worried our financial markets into depression.

It was all fairly complicated to me, so as a child I asked God to help. In my young mind, I thought this would start to fix the world that was on the brink of annihilation, and prove He was real and still cared for us.

Over the next few years, I recalled the initial prayer once in awhile, especially when something reminded me that we were living under a *nuclear umbrella*. Even though I wasn't aware of it, God was not only planning to answer this child's prayer along with the millions of others who desperately called out to Him for mercy; he was going to take a corn-fed Catholic boy along for the ride!

Even up to the point when President Ronald Reagan stood at the Brandenburg Gate in Berlin and told the Soviet Premier to, "...tear down this wall!" I didn't think it would happen in my lifetime. After all, it was a huge empire and the wall was thick reinforced concrete, their symbol of defiance against the West. I was afraid to believe in such a quick answer to my childhood prayer. Realized requests from God will scare you at first. Yet, it's critical to discover the faith of a child can move mountains.

I was truly burdened by this prayer and its ramifications during my entire adolescent and early adult life. It all seemed like a dream. Only my wife knew about the significance of the prayer, as she was close enough to experience the commitment with me. Our children were small and went along on my journey without understanding what their parents were doing to support the cause.

We followed Ronald Reagan's vision closely and he never disappointed us. I remember stopping in a grocery store parking lot and listening to President Reagan's radio message to the nation, which was similar to my prayer. What arrogance or lunacy was this? How could I be part of this man's vision before it was ever presented and what gave us the right to hope for a solution? *Détente, appeasement, negotiations, treaties* were the buzzword solutions from intellectuals.

As proud as I was of our idealistic leader, their silky couture dressed our national doubts in comfortable stylized concepts to thwart Reagan's ability to crush the evil monster of communism. But I was with him. My wife and I sent his election and re-election campaigns money. We prayed consistently for his leadership to be guided by divine influence over world events.

As early donors, our names are among several hundred printed on a courtyard wall at the Ronald Reagan Republican

Center in Washington D.C. A few years ago, we went to see the wall and it brought all the memories back like a flood upon my brain. How could our simple support register as it did? I couldn't believe the power of my little prayer as I stood at the shrine to renewed freedom, birthed many years earlier and carried to fruition by millions of liberty loving people.

In 1981, an opportunity to do more than send money arose. I was recalled to active military duty as one of only 10 people selected nation wide to help train the tens of thousands of new Air Force troops needed at the start of the Reagan military build up. *The 10* were to complete one, three-year tour and then return to *weekend-warrior* status. God had only begun to show me His wisdom. It was time for radical change in my young life—time to live by faith or die in spirit.

During our tour of duty in Boot Camp, I volunteered to attend Officer Training School to be a Nuclear Missile Launch Officer. Learning first hand how this was the primary weapon system the Soviets respected enough to give it their undivided attention, helped destroy my ignorance of nuclear war.

After missile duty, I was detoured to aircraft maintenance. Mr. Reagan's plans for persuading Soviet communists to capitulate included showing them our newest long-range bomber capabilities. Again, God was putting me in a place where I could see what it takes to answer prayers. In this case, our B-1 Bombers could answer "Peace through Strength," in a moments notice. When I actively participated in the solution, I saw my prayer answered and understood the path.

From the pointy end of the spear, I could observe our Cold War efforts. However, lacking open source evidence of the Soviet demise fueled popular sentiment against the fight. The protest of hopelessness bore down on us like a lead pellet pillow pressing harder as each year passed, threatening to smother our very existence. Winning the Cold War became risky and like a heavyweight-boxing match, both weary combatants, tired and desperate, used innate skills near the finish to KO its rival. In the end only one battle worn *super power*, which always returns to its roots, remained standing.

The world is very different today. We don't consider the possibility of annihilation by nuclear weapons or economic ruin from overspending on a military build up. We enjoy relative comfort and prosperity and take it all for granted. Yet, it was not like that 25 years ago. After a decade of our absolute faith and perseverance in a righteous endeavor, the *evil empire* ceased to exist just as President Reagan said it would.

Through President Reagan's guiding, "Trust but Verify" model, we did the unthinkable. After 45 years of retreating, decades of failed foreign policies, and years of selecting incompetent leaders, we happened upon a real American spirit and hired him to see us through our own folly. This man was after God's own heart. He was a poet-warrior—an example of the kind of leader America produces when artist, patriot and piety come together. His character was simple and complex coexisting inside a well-read, trained and disciplined freedom loving man. He had been fighting the same devil for over forty years and knew exactly what it would take to win.

If we really want something, God will allow it to happen with our involvement. The next time weary events take hold of your life, remember—you asked for it! A big house, brilliant and considerate children, world peace... How are we to recognize God's help if we don't directly observe the process or see the things that produce results?

I found out long ago that reading the newspaper or listening to the nightly news would not reveal God's plan for each of us. If you want miracles, get ready for a roller coaster ride. If you want unending entertainment to mask troubles, stay home and watch TV or glue yourself to the Internet. It's safe and sorry.

See what faith in prayer, patience, persistence and participation can do? The rest of the world by now has figured out how we won the Cold War. They adopted the naive notions of pundits, as hindsight clarifies their reasoning. But President Reagan knew it would take a lot of hard work, faith, and trust in God answering many prayers, to win this victory over evil.

The ugly giant shook his shield, brandished his sword, and fumed hateful invitations to make war. The huge Soviet Empire wasn't counting on a couple of boys from Illinois with faith and prayers coming after them. Like Sir Winston Churchill once said, *"Never give in, never give in, never, never, never, never; in nothing great or small, large or petty, never give in!"*

Looking back, I can see God's glory in my prayer. He was going to free the Eastern Block countries without me, but my prayer let Him know I was ready for the truth. The greatest gift a warrior can receive is *inclusion in the solution.* The loftier the problem, the grander the victory even though small steps are required to realize the gain. Having family to share the burdens, sacrifices and memories makes it worthwhile.

What a ride I had! Knowing the truth about one of the greatest mysteries of our time is more valuable than gold to me. To understand how a boy's heartfelt prayer, turned into a man's experience of a world on the brink of destruction, gives concordance to heart and mind. Do I believe that walls can come tumbling down? You bet! Even though the band stopped playing long ago, I can still hear the victory music. I heed the throngs of jubilant voices, cheering the words of one brave man of vision, and I remember every line he spoke.

Sometimes in a moment of reflection on the 1980s, the flag seems to wave braver, and our liberty rings truer. My heels come together as my body straightens to attention and I salute the fresh free breeze of American Spirit. I pray that more people find it, and that enough remember what it took to secure the blessings of liberty we all enjoy, to sustain the dream. May God bless America as we abide in Him.

"There is one sign the Soviets can make that would be unmistakable, that would advance dramatically the cause of freedom and peace. General Secretary Gorbachev, if you seek peace, if you seek prosperity for the Soviet Union and Eastern Europe, if you seek liberalization, come to this gate! Mr. Gorbachev, open this gate. Mr. Gorbachev, *tear down this wall!*"

President Ronald Reagan
(1911 - 2004)

40th President
Of the United States of America

Speech at the Brandenburg Gate
West Berlin, June 12, 1987

Paradox Dedication

I dedicate *Paradox* to Ryan David Engle. May you find need in the longing for such a prayer that reveals God's presence now and all the days of your life. Pass onto your children the power of faith in our living God made human through Jesus Christ and made manifest through the Holy Spirit. Through Him the big gets very small and the small makes all the difference in the world.

With God's Grace,
Jeff

The glory of young men is their strength,
And the splendor of old men is their gray hair.

Proverbs 20:29

Paradox
(on life)

A paradox of the mind.
The soul is left empty, when experience is
Trusted to children, faith based on adult status.

Dichotomy, perhaps dangerous some say.
Yet, complex subjects crumble just as
Mature mortar begins its timely decay.

Lethargy of confident mind confides:
"Build a life on childishness,
Practice a sacred, solid, pleasure filled world."
A strong wind or rain just might tornado,
And blow it all away.

But child like faith in heaven, and adult practice in life,
Begets a good foundation, travesty cannot crush.
Bring unto me the children...
He spoke of child like faith.

Wealth through the needle's eye,
A camel would more likely fit.
Describes His contempt for common cultural accouterments,
Which burden faith, and shrink the souls of men.

Rather, be a child in heart for God.
Take satisfaction in pleasuring His Will,
And find the place legends are made of,
To sustain your winged ascent into eternity.

Newborn Narrative

"We have it in our power to begin the world over again."
Thomas Paine, American Patriot

This poem just burst forth while I was listening to some national election rhetoric on the broadcast news. I used to yell at the TV during political seasons. Now, I mostly stop watching and substitute reading history. I added the last four stanzas when my fifth grandchild, Riley Owen Bair, entered the world. This verse is metaphor for the birth of our nation as it portends a union with the offspring who inherit a world of our works.

Newborn suggests an innocent entering the world with its cry for affection and needs ignored by pop-political discretion. A wiser nation would consider her cries an asset to its existence. This shows a dichotomous rift between what is more significant: a new soul's arrival on earth, or the gamesmanship of our conjured societal import.

A cynical culture rejects even the obvious innocent behavior of a helpless newborn baby. Callous minds and hardened hearts scrutinize its small voice of hurt, hunger, and loneliness. The antipathy for trust in a living God grinds humanity into a course aggregate used to mortar the next wall of rationalized deism, separating us further from His intended joy.

The babe is tolerated by discerning opinions as if it was in their power to grant such acceptance in the first place. Who lobbies for the weakest among us? What powerful group insures the rights of a newborn are guarded even as she rests a helpless soul inside her mother's womb?

"We hold these truths to be self evident: that all men are created equal; that they are endowed by their Creator with certain inalienable rights; that among these are life, liberty and

the pursuit of happiness." (The Committee of Five, drafters of the Declaration of Independence, 1776).

Inalienable means: *not transferable to another person,* and incapable of being: *denied, rejected or disowned;* without regard to: *disapproval, divorce, shame, disavowing,* and cannot be: *renounced, discarded or disclaimed.*

This is a great responsibility as well as a burden awaiting the unsuspecting newborn. No wonder she is crying! Yet, how many of us realize that we share the weight of this basic political concept that sets us apart from the rest of human history? The Declaration of Independence is our nation's birth certificate. Every freedom we enjoy came from the first American document that reads like poetry and strikes at the heart of tyranny like iron. The Bill of Rights and our Constitution are held in place by this formidable document's foundational reality.

We are tasked with defending our right to live against tolerance, ignorance, apathy and indifference. James Madison, our fourth President, insured that the word *tolerance* was left out of the Virginia Declaration of Rights used by Thomas Jefferson to flesh out the United States Declaration of Independence draft. In his biography of Madison, author Ralph Ketcham explains, quoting Thomas Paine: *tolerance* [as it is related to religious freedom], *"not the opposite of intolerance, but...the counterfeit of it. Both are despotisms. The one* [intolerance] *assumes to itself the right of withholding liberty of conscience, the other* [tolerance] *of granting it."*

Determinism, on the other hand, holds that *everything* is fixed by forces outside of our control, allowing for excuse to behave anyway one wishes while affording *tolerance* for others behavior based on their inability to control *anything.*

This ill-conceived notion prevails in the minds and actions of a wide audience that run counter to the underpinnings of American values. It is pervasive, enticing and a failed model.

Liberty means individual choice, freedom from another's control or obligation regardless of any bias or prejudice we or anyone else might have. It is a reciprocal right among God's human creations. Adding *tolerance* to its definition prescribes someone holding power over another and allowing them to participate in society under certain conditions. We must remain vigilant applying the lessons of hard fought and sacrificially won liberties. We are obligated to educate and define our freedoms, one generation to the next.

Happiness is another word for joy. And that is the real test for the newborn soul. Will the *pursuit of happiness* lead to discovering the joy God allows? Does our young nation continue to practice the basic principles laid out by its well-informed Founders with their same force of liberty, and trust in the Spirit of 1776? Or do we succumb to common-sense illusion from power hungry wolves in sheep's wrappings.

We can tinker with the United States Constitution but *not* the Declaration of Independence. Our way of life, government and civilization is based on these small, yet powerful, principles: We are **created** and **equal**; not evolved and tolerated. We are given universal rights by our Creator among which *life, liberty and the pursuit of happiness* are most important. And those *truths* are evidential in nature.

Logic dictates that if you are not able to accept these precepts as defining your homeland, then freedom allows you to choose another place to live, renounce citizenship, or start your own country. As long as the Declaration of Independence stands as the seminal instrument for building this new nation, *good sense* will not allow us to turn our backs on its dictum. Its truism is not just an acceptable offering. It is a requirement of our citizenship: a right, which cannot be denied—a law written poetically to capture all human spirit, while demanding attention and commanding loyalty from every person under its sovereignty.

The infant viewing areas in hospitals seem to be woefully empty. Maybe my infrequent visits just happen upon a spell of low birthrate. Yet, I can't help feeling sad when the clear plastic bassinets are empty. Raising children trumps all other endeavors. It outlasts our finest accomplishments. As a grandparent, I'm comforted by the arrival of new babies who will grow to continue the work started by their parents and improve our world.

A new generation affords hope to the last; that lessons learned will be remembered, added like yeast to fresh bread so that a new society can rise to its potential. The allure of cynicism will fade into transcendent events as the past awakens hearts and minds, the present rejects denial of truth, and the future holds promise for the rebirth of liberty, and trust in God—like a newborn baby's first breath cries out for compassion and inalienable human rights.

"I am apt to believe that it will be celebrated, by succeeding Generations, as the great anniversary Festival. It ought to be commemorated...with Pomp and Parade, with Shows, Games, Sports, Guns, Bells, Bonfires and Illuminations from one End of this Continent to the other. From this Time forward forever more."

**John Adams
(1735 -1826)**

Second President
First Vice President
Of the United States of America

Member—Committee of Five
On the Declaration of Independence

To Abigail Adams
July 3, 1776

Newborn Dedication

I dedicate *Newborn* to my third grandson, Riley Owen Bair. Your birth inspired new text and added meaning to old notions that need remembered. May you always seek the truth and not give in to sensational information as a guide. So you will be an inspiration to many, which I pray never lose their desire for hearing, seeing, and reading the truth as it exists through God's laws and principles.

Love,

Grandpa Bair

For the Lord gives wisdom;
from his mouth come knowledge and understanding.

Proverbs 2:6

Newborn

Newborn baby's cries,
Belie unscrupulous lies,
Cynical minds try to deny.

"Blind raging blast blaze heat these days,"
A sledge swinging satirist surly says.
"From whence came thou wisdom blest?"
I worked hard for it, like all the rest.

Must be earned, it cannot be given,
Should guard it fresh, with each new generation.
It's ours to live, not take away nor deny Freedom;
Sharpened tools, from the past, when we need them.

Creaky chest of ancient words opens laden,
With treasures rich in solemn oaths they had taken.
Why such fondness of things gone, when they are hazy?
Most valued cache hidden from lame, weak and lazy.

Down-trodden lot, forget us not, this message always.
We came and saw, and fought for all, in past days.
Now live and play, in better ways, than we could render,
So you will know, which way to grow, without surrender.

As life goes on, a paragon of mortals triumph.
Maladies of broken dreams mend,
From wisdom's ointment.

When civilization slumbers,
Or vagrant lumbers,
In foggy recess,
Return to glory, in our first story, with victory and success!

The Lie Narrative

The model is simple. Few people comprehend; Treat money like a hobby and Truth like a friend.   Author

I just about fell out of my chair at a retirement get-together when the new commanding general started off his remarks with, "You know one man's truth is another man's lie..."

He launched into a tirade about cutbacks, Congress and I don't know what all. I stopped listening and felt embarrassed for him, pitied the rest of us, and felt sorry for that poor guy who was supposed to be getting a hardy hale and farewell before we kicked him out the door with a discounted pension.

But there it was, in my face again, another common saying someone presses via his position, influencing others to accept. Am I supposed to follow this guy? I must admit I once tried to live this way, listening to popular over-simplifications of life's struggles while complicating God's requirements for joy.

It's an awakening to accept truth. Once awake, it is wrong to accept the lies anymore, even though your job or relationships may count on them. That's when you begin to feel alone and persecution begins. It's then, that the grace of God can lift you up to see above the fog of war. It's this realization of His grace that sustains your existence among the living dead.

We must only die once; live in truth and depart this life into glory. The truth does set you free and he who is set free by believing in Jesus Christ and repenting of sin, is free indeed.

"They say the world has become too complex for simple answers. They are wrong. There are no *easy* answers, but there are *simple* answers. We must have courage to do what we know is morally right."

Ronald Reagan (1911-2004)
Goldwater Speech, October 27, 1964

The Lie Dedication

Dedicating this to one person would just not be right. Let's all take a piece of this one and chew on it for awhile. I pray that as God continues to reveal Himself to our wondering minds, we learn to trust in His truth and not condemn the Word that flows through men as favored by the holy text. May we realize the misguided mockery of these holy words and meanings is common cultural interpretation of truth, and lies. God is love and light, Christ is truth and the Holy Spirit will grace us with all understanding.

Jeff

The law of the Lord is perfect, converting the soul;
The testimony of the Lord is sure making wise the simple.

Psalm 19:7

If you abide in My word, you are my disciples indeed.
And you shall know the truth,
and the truth shall make you free.

John 8:31-32

The Lie

"One man's truth is another man's lie,"
  The old man said to me.
He backed it up with his credentials,
  By any measure, successfully.

His words fell like ripe fruit,
  Dull thud upon my brain.
The lie was not one man's truth,
  But what he should not say.

Conveniently placed morality,
  Efficacious kind to buy.
Too common for the spirit,
  And casual in the mind.

Oh, heart be troubled daily,
  ·Slings and arrows must receive.
If only to be narrow,
  Soul's truth left to believe.

While men's words can never hold,
  A postulate for prayer.
The Spirit beckons reason!
  A truth, none can despair.

As sure as they will speak it,
  More surely it will twist.
There truly is no judgment,
  Morality less than this.

Be on your guard as men speak,
  For they are all endowed;
With willing words of wisdom,
  Picked especially for the crowd.

Great need and longing reason,
  To trust one *Healing Word.*
For it exists unfettered,
  By desperate kneeling world.

The Way Narrative

"Subtle is the LORD, yet malicious is He not."
Albert Einstein, carved in Princeton University mantel.

This poem wrote itself. Not much needed changing. My struggle with faith was finally tipping in the right direction. I had entertained so many philosophies on life and tested all sorts of creeds. I was weary of looking. The search must end.

I believe God reveals Himself and His reason for creating us through His Word, answers to our prayers, observable nature and His flesh and blood Son, Jesus of Nazareth.

When things got bad or very difficult throughout my life, I always asked for divine intervention. As a Catholic, I prayed to saints, Mary and Joseph (the mother and adoptive father of Jesus). As a youth, I used to sing hymns along cold and lonely streets. This would sustain me until I got into a warm place.

Now, I talk to God frequently and ask for continued grace and mercy. This comes by way of His Son's sacrifice; that which makes us acceptable to Him. This calms the anxieties of life like a reassuring close friend. He continues to reveal Himself in the truth of His laws and commands. I find miracles pour forth like warm rain on my thirsty face. It overwhelms me sometimes and I cry. After a while, I realize it was Him answering another prayer.

I know this because I recollect my asking. By staying aware of God's answers, you can habituate the practice of **Problem, Prayer, and Place**, waiting for the change to happen.

We always begin with a *problem*. Even an atheist will say a *prayer* for God's help if the trouble is desperate enough. The practiced believer prays all the time and knows how to recognize the time and *place* of God's answer. Doubt disappears and glory goes back to Him. The process begins over everyday, until it becomes nourishment to our faith, and sustenance to a joy-filled life.

As people enjoy good food, the believer prepares a meal of good prayer before the Lord as an offering in faith. God always accepts our potluck prayers, invites us to dine with Him and satisfies our hungry and thirsty souls.

Constantly seeking physical stimulation and pleasure, will not satisfy; it will consume our hearts, minds, bodies and souls. There is no joy in any of that. There is simply distraction from the obvious need of our soul to learn and grow, so it will know, which way to go, when the body no longer holds it captive.

The longer we participate in pleasure seeking, the further we get away from love, truth and joy! Occasional gratifying stimulus is healthy, but if it turns into obsession, making life duller, then we must consider the activity harmful to finding our way out of a dark battle zone.

Remember, the ancient Romans were famous for escalating all types of benign activities into binges of uncontrolled self indulgences. Is our culture mimicking the unsatisfied thrill seeking that fallen civilizations once abided? The adult must take over and moderate our behavior.

Stop for awhile. Quiet your mind. Turn off the TV (trust me, you won't miss it!). Read a good book (cover-to-cover) about healthy ideas. Do this often and reflect on the brain cells exercised in this activity versus those dulled through easy, scripted contrivances from our statistically led, human nature studied, profile driven, commercially callused, culturally corrected, cranked out, humanistic pleasure machines.

Begin to find *the way* to life that has you smiling without realizing it, and that makes you comfortable in a world created for you to experience and enjoy. My warrior heart finds abundant joy in victory over the forces of darkness. Perhaps your joy will find you in another manner. Ask God to show you *The Way*.

The Way Dedication

May I dedicate this one to myself? With your indulgence, I pray you forgive what may appear to be self-serving. I wrote this one for me. I need to see His Face someday. Like my prayers in the past, I know God will answer this one. Once again, I rely on Jesus to tell me why God does it. I simply reflect on having made the prayer when I needed help. Remember: *Problem, Prayer, Place!*

Jeffrey

Jesus said to him, "I am The Way, The Truth, and The Life. No one comes to the Father except through Me.

John 14:6

The Way

I did ascend into a mist,
  A fog of blank despair.
And while I groped at formlessness,
  A spirit white appeared.

His shape was perfect to my eye,
  Until he turned around.
There on his gold trimmed tunic frame,
  Five open wounds I found.

Fear not, He said, *For in thy haste,*
  You passed by solid ground.
And as He spoke the fog did lift,
  So I could look around.

A charming field of flowers bloomed,
  Blue, purple, yellow blend.
My heart was light and unentombed,
  I asked my new found friend.

"Lord, it was dark but now it's light,
  Pray tell from where this came?"
Remember when I promised life,
  If only you had faith.

Your trust at last has lifted you,
  Up to a higher plain.
And now you live eternally,
  In Heaven with Me again.

Part 3

Soft Lessons

A Taste of Honey

If *Part 2* felt like a bump in the road to joy, *Part 3* is the down hill run. You'll notice I begin with the big three: **Wisdom, Courage** and **Serenity**, to which all my prayers are anchored.

Needing to abandon foolish behavior, I first prayed for *wisdom*. When I was confused between wisdom and inaction, I prayed for *courage* to press on into uncharted waters. Finally, worried about pride getting in the way of God's plans, I prayed for *serenity* to quiet my mind in order to hear and see God's messages. By concentrating on one thing at a time, I learned to focus on my problems.

Normally, I'm an erratic child. Focus is a chore sometimes and other times I must pull myself away from an issue. Fortunately, I've had world-class discipline instruction called *Basic Training*. Most people only need 6 to 12 weeks of basic training to get their priorities straight—I needed three years of it.

My first dive into the icy cold pool of military style discipline came as a trainee in 1975. Later, from July 1981 to May 1984, I served as an MTI (Air Force Equivalent of an Army or Marine drill instructor). I've always believed that basic training would make a good non-dependency alternative to child and adolescent mood altering drugs, popularly prescribed by doctors, for the benefit of parents and teachers.

I still struggle with the heebie-jeebies getting my dander up from time-to-time. A good swift return to basics, a dose of self-rebuke, prayer and a lot of mercy puts me back on the narrow path. I am a child in faith, and believe God provides for His children a future filled with increasing joy as long as they discipline themselves as adults and follow His rules.

As with all God's blessings, joy comes in the morning. Often hard work, trials and discipline open our eyes to the price we must pay to enjoy victory. Through victory, we renew strength in the Holy Spirit, crossing obstacles to joy on earth. In rising to the battle, the adult knows how to win.

When I was young, I went to visit a seminary to contemplate a life for Christ as a Roman Catholic priest. The adults in my life refused to send me back to complete high school there for reasons I still don't know. I was ready for the priesthood then, but I thank God for His blessings in my life now. These uncontrolled directions in destiny can help us find God's purpose for our lives, while returning honor and glory to Him.

Looking back, it is much easier to see the sense in my life's direction than trying to mold the future. The lack of vision into our future requires faith in something to guide our footsteps. Without the guide, we will miss experiencing fully His intention for our life. Fortunately, we can always get back to the meaning of life by accepting God's Will through faith, sustained by prayer. He is always faithful to us if we abide and seek His help. It is *never* too late to embrace the Gospel.

Joy does exist. It can be a giddy feeling that tickles your heart, mind and spirit. However, I find it dynamic and deeper than mere emotions. To me, joy is like the serious side of happiness. Why did our American founding fathers consider the "...pursuit of Happiness" important enough to include in our foundational deed to freedom?

They were learned men from all walks of life. Various styles of living and religious faiths were represented in their negotiations over our "more perfect union." Happiness is another word for joy, and God ordained that we discover, "unspeakable joy" (1 Peter 1:8).

Truth reveals itself through candid assessment of observable constants. Adding an acceptance of things popularly considered awkward, silly, and soft, we truly learn to live. Absorb the nectar of the next few pages, and refresh your appetite often. You'll find herein pleasant rhyme on which to feed your mind, heart and soul. Our minds are weak, our hearts puny, and souls are undernourished. Eat of this fruit often. It costs nothing, asks nothing in return, and best of all is non-fattening.

I hope you enjoy this next section. It's a montage of rededication. As I read these verses, I'm reminded that someone must have been praying for me. That is a great blessing. It takes discipline and love beyond common understanding to pray for someone else. Try it and see how He answers prayer.

Joy is the product of picking and choosing to live a certain lifestyle—harnessing the harvest of God's full measure of blessings He intended for us. When joy comes, bang the keys of your calliope. Send up a joyful noise in praise of Him who loves you. Remember to reflect on how you got to where joy enters your heart, mind and soul. Practice the methods described here and in the Word of God, repeatedly. Joy is food for the soul. Feed your soul and trust it will grow—to lift you heaven bound in your day of glory.

"Few men have virtue to withstand the highest bidder."

George Washington
(1732 - 1799)

First President
of the United States of America

Dedication of Part 3

I dedicate Part 3 to my sister Mary. Your smile reminds me of childhood days; a sunny warm summer stroll in Miller Park with a snow cone waiting for us in the old log cabin refreshment stand. May God bless and keep you in His loving mercy and bless your countenance with light, as joy is present in your heart.

Love,
Jeff

Only a simpleton believes everything he's told!
A prudent man understands the need for proof.
A wise man is cautious and avoids danger;
A fool plunges ahead with great confidence.

Proverbs 14:15-16

Wisdom Narrative

My first prayer was for wisdom. It is clear that I was asking God to bestow a gift greater than wealth, greater than health, and more than I deserved. I asked Him repeatedly for it. Then life began to change. My decisions were no longer popular with people around me. Criticism grew from every move made, as I learned to fear the LORD instead of fearing those whose opinions rise like scalding steam to soak and dampen spirit. Their judgment only hurts if you get close enough to the searing humid air of brazen conjecture to let it flush your emotions red with blisters. Otherwise, step away and be safe.

A tenuous balance between appeasing perception and living in truth overhauls our mind's requisite for excellence. We subordinate God's gift of rational reason to contrived correctness just to *get along* with the crowd around us; maybe it's at work, play, church, school, volunteering, home, in a relationship or while our opinions and intellect are being formed.

It takes courage to lean on faith in God, while accepting change to embrace the revolution required within us to begin anew. We will look at the virtue *courage* in the next narrative.

Wondering more than once if I was going mad, encouraged fear to tempt me into believing the external world was hostile. I finally realized this new sensitivity was persecution. What gave me the right to behave differently from my sinful ways? I began to withdraw from making personal decisions. Then Jesus' Cross-revealed showed me the love of his accepted abuse to overcome the reality of my sin and His death, on my behalf.

Becoming a coward means hiding, and suffering the lowest form of human disgrace. Wisdom was becoming a burden. It would have been easier to obtain and held on to it earlier in life. But I was asking for it now when unfamiliar surroundings vexed my spirit and I felt that I did not deserve God's blessings. After much prayer, Christ's victory entered my heart.

Like other good things in God's image, wisdom is worth all the effort and sacrifice to receive and maintain. Over time, it grows like a pumpkin. Its color is pleasant, but not flashy or easily rhymed with popular rhetoric. Its taste is bitter until sweetened by love, and spiced with triumph. Its weight can become a real burden to carry as it grows in the fertile soil of decaying sin, parasitic weaknesses and loamy transgressions.

Through wisdom, new kinds of people begin to share life with you who are servants to humanity, emulating our Creator's superior love. My flaws from ignorance stun most people because an otherwise excellent appearance can be such a waste of human potential without wisdom. Pray for wisdom, to learn from mistakes experienced or from the acts of people in the Bible. "The fear of the LORD *is* the beginning of wisdom." Proverbs 9:10. Evidence of acquired wisdom comes from persecution, while freedom from tragic mistake reveals God's glory through it and through you.

I'm on the right path now and the quest continues for me. If you want to join my journey, you'll have to get in front of, or behind me. The path is getting narrower, and my progress slowed by carrying the weight of a growing pumpkin. I can barely see my own footsteps, and only one at a time. God talks to me in *serenity*, while His angels show themselves in small ways that only spiced faith and growing wisdom, can perceive.

"Did blind chance know that there was light and what was its refraction, and fit the eyes of all creatures after the most curious manner to make use of it? These and other suchlike considerations, always have, and always will prevail with mankind, to believe that there is a Being who made all things, who has all things in His power, and who is therefore to be feared."

Sir Isaac Newton
(1642-1727)
English mathematician, physicist, philosopher

Wisdom Dedication

I dedicate *Wisdom* to my first grandson, Silas Jeffrey Bair. May you always walk in the ways of the Lord Jesus Christ and find wisdom early in life. So that all your days will be filled with blessings from God and He will find you of His own heart.

Love,
Grandpa Bair

Behold! You desire truth in the inward parts,
and in the hidden part You will make me to know Wisdom.

Psalm 51:6

Wisdom

This door opens to a magical place,
  Of ancient tales and anecdotal rhymes.
The likes of which men elusively chase,
  From past, through proud present, to future times.

If enter ye here, know well ye this toast,
  For most moil on, to find treasures in vain.
"May all eat fruit grown, from fertile compost,
  When dullness dies, and apathy is slain."

So enter ye now, while fresh face doth kiss,
  Beyond this broad breach, great wealth ye will find.
Sturdy hearts toil long, at tasks less than this,
  While the Wise, use keys faithful, to their minds.

Courage Narrative

"Courage is fear that has said its prayers."
Dorothy Bernard (1890–1955)
Silent Movie Actress

Studying the history of human warfare for many years, led to writing this poem. The ranks of living, breathing, panicked and impassioned, numb and weary soldiers were in my mind. They seemed to speak to me a general impression of their courageous character as mostly mistaken. Other forces like fear, friendship, faith, and focused discipline held warriors together in perilous times to aid in a heroic or tragic event.

Young and old, weak and strong, educated and ignorant marched together, mile after grueling mile, through torturous weather, plagued by disease and hunger, often, to reach an end to their life's journey. The place and time of their demise was chosen by another, with little regard for the warrior's purpose on earth, except as fodder for the beast of war. A hundred maladies tugged at ragged clothed bodies, with hunger wrenching empty bellies while the dogs of fatigue nipped at their soar heels, only to end in bloody conflict.

My meaning is not to slight anyone who sacrificed his all, for our country. I once hovered close to death myself in a military mission, and understand the threat. Somehow, my fear was abated by companionship of admirable comrades. I did my duty for our country's causes and marched at least a thousand miles in military formations. Hot and wringing with sweat, or cold and damp, we marched side by side to a military cadence.

I enjoy reading books or watching good movies about our American heroes. I visit their memorials and battle fields as often as I can. I pray to be worthy of their sacrifices.

The ancient soldiers are on my mind often. We love them for their selflessness, but they want us to know a different kind of courage exists. It is the courage to change, to pursue long-suffering battles of human kindness, charity, and love for one another, accountability and vigilance for freedom.

A colonel of mine once said, "...don't ever tell me you're comfortable!" This confused me at the time, but now I understand what he meant. The battle is always with us. The enemy constantly seeks our slumber. When we rest too long we get comfy-cozy and become easy victims for powers of darkness. It's good to exercise our minds, hearts and bodies to stay alert.

In David McCullough's biography of John Adams, we learn our second President walked 3 to 10 miles nearly every day of his life, and rode a horse into his eighties! Mr. Adams was the first and best example of the dedicated American public servant. He exemplified an idealistic spirit which persisted until righteous causes were complete. Then, without any aggrandizement, he left public life with a legacy of service and sacrifice that continues today in many of our public professionals. John Adams had the heart of a poet-warrior. He was a nation builder of the highest order.

I pray for a modern awakening to these values intended to inculcate courage into the fabric of our society. Our American founding fathers made *a more perfect union* for us to enjoy, nourish, refine and improve upon. They are not just, "dead white men!" They shared the vision with all races, ethnic groups, and creeds. They involved both genders in the recipe for America and admit being led by the will of virtuous women. They epitomized familial unity with strength in kindred spirit. They suffered greatly for the start of our nation.

A people divided by the sin of slavery still found common ground to coexist under a new thesis of unanimity until their false reality ignoring the nexus of evil among them, required a bloody conflict to resolve the obvious mistake. It was simple, but not easy to deal with in peace. Finally, the failing was settled in terms of terrible civil war and human anguish of biblical proportions.

We must not fall prey to embracing comfort over courage. Go back into any history and find slavery throughout the world in obvious and subtle forms from Israelites to Africans, or child labor to abused wives and husbands. You can find tyranny in landowner over sharecropper, professor over student, management over labor, political party over ignorant constituency or government over citizens. Power practiced for personal gain ends in humiliation for the proud. Personal pride deadens our hearts to the voice of Spirit led reason. Group pride needs emolument from virtuous leaders who know how to build spirit without losing modesty. The servant leader, like Adams, satisfies our Creator's likeness in us.

The enemy is still out there prowling like a lion that never rests. Wake up! Be courageous now and everyday or support someone who is spirited. Let us not be taken captive and deprived of freedom by any form of overt or subtle slavery now that we hold the elemental riches of *Life, Liberty and the pursuit of Happiness;* born of freedom, paid for in blood, and sustained through *courage.* WAKE UP NOW!

"Once more unto the breach, dear friends, once more; or close the wall up with our English dead! In peace there's nothing so becomes a man as modest stillness and humility: But when the blast of war blows in our ears, then imitate the action of the tiger; Stiffen the sinews, summon up the blood, disguise fair nature with hard-favored rage; Then lend the eye a terrible aspect."

**William Shakespeare
(1564-1616)**

Henry V, Act: III, Scene 1

Courage Dedication

I dedicate *Courage* to the memory of the late Jonathan Chamberlain of the famed U.S. Civil War Christian Commission, and to the men and women of the modern Military Ministry who portray John Chamberlain's charitable qualities. Also, to John Wega, who depicts Jonathan Chamberlain in a contemporary Christian Commission at Gettysburg, PA, and Bryan Crawmer who retells, accurately, the great United States Civil War story—may God bless you and yours, for living courageously by passing along His laws and principles so that others might live a joy filled life.

Your friend,
Jeff

*"Be strong and of good courage,
do not fear nor be afraid of them;
for the Lord your God,
He is the one who goes with you.
He will not leave you nor forsake you."*

Deuteronomy 31:6

Courage

What courage we, whose lifeblood soaked into the ground?
We simply swelled war ranks in time to learn to pray.
Who fought for colored cloth, dipped to a martial sound,
While the living, fight indifference, still today.

Why courage we, in harm's way saved ours in decease?
Where courage those who dared injustice fight and live.
With courage some lead, fighting for eternal peace;
When easier a martyr's selflessness, to give.

All courage comes from faith, and skill, and supple heart,
Strong will, just cause, compassion, healthy noble mind.
For in all scribed histories ever man did chart,
Most courageous those in faith, serve all mankind.

Serenity Narrative

It was difficult to get my mind around this poem. At the time, there was a popular return in movies to medieval subjects. I admit having a fascination with Arthur Pendragon and Knights of the Round Table, Excalibur, Chivalry, Knights Templar and the like. Once, I was a *Knight of the Altar* as an acolyte in church services. The first book I ever checked out of the old town library was *Ivanhoe*, by Sir Walter Scott.

God didn't make man for decision making and battle fighting alone. A third element requires silent reflection in order for wisdom and courage to succeed. God gave us the capacity to quiet our thoughts from words and deeds to allow us to hear His voice. Our poet-warrior president, Lincoln, sought after serenity to answer enormous questions of battle, discipline and power, tempered by tenderness of human compassion, and strengthened by prayer's ascent through the Spirit of the LORD. Like Lincoln, in weakness, we are made strong.

How quiet the Last Supper room must have been when Jesus raised his cup and told the disciples about His blood that was about to be poured out for them. When bread, like His body, was broken couldn't they hear, as well as see it rip apart?

Serenity must have surrounded them in the first few seconds after His resurrection appearance. The disciples took strength from this tranquility as each passed through trials, torture and death. Without serenity, we cannot hear the voice of God; His truth and loving rebuke of our transgressions, and we risk His scorn or wrath. Therefore, learn to listen in quiet solitude. Here's to your health, a toast from the Grail of Eternal Life!

"I have been driven many times to my knees by the overwhelming conviction that I had nowhere else to go. My own wisdom, and that of all about me, seemed insufficient for the day."

Abraham Lincoln (1809-1865)

Serenity Dedication

I dedicate *Serenity* to my late grandparents Paul and Loretta Thoennes. By your loving manner, I learned to quiet my voice, enjoy silence and open my mind to thinking and praying. May God hold you in His loving care until I see you again in Heaven.

Love,
Jeff

Finally brethren, farewell. Become complete.
Be of good comfort, be of one mind, live in peace;
and the God of love and peace will be with you.

2 Corinthians 13:11

Serenity

A flower kept fragrant, from sense-filled search,
  Elemental gold most men rarely held.
Its petals pride peels like leathery birch,
  When hot temper frustrates delicate weld.

Onward feet must stride; this journey is right,
  Though thorny trials rip at armor and mail.
'Till naked standing alone in the light,
  Bowed and bruised by bludgeoning in the flail.

Bright moon lights not white, broad path's sudden gloom,
  Gaunt cheeks deeply cut by challenging blade.
Nocturnal abyss moans, *"Down to your doom."*
  While longing stammers, "If only I'd stayed."

Lord, please tell me why, I fear more than most,
  And why my mind thinks it knows right from wrong?
Tranquil subjects I seek, always to host,
  While a righteous grip, slips surely along.

To hear and obey is the only way,
  My presence, for you, to know and to feel.
In truth, I am among you whilst you pray,
  My Spirit, in solemn silence, will heal.

Platinum sails billow bright on pale blue,
  The power to move them real but unseen.
I swear by my soul this quest to be true,
  Thus, to your health! From the Cup! of—Serene.

I Know Love Well Narrative

This is a free form verse I hope you enjoy reading over and over again. It truly is my heart talking to my head. We can become better lovers of life, God, and His Creation. We can have more excellent affection for each other, our work, learning, and of joy. We need to remember our existence is in the image of our Creator and He is love. We are being used by Him for a greater purpose. Abiding in this knowledge affords us great power over darkness, and grants us real wealth in living. Saving up these gifts fills our being with vital energy.

This thing called love is probably God's most complex gift to us. Yet, He allows us to enjoy its rewards through simple faith. Hardened hearts do not live, they merely survive.

The dualities of big and little, love and hate, lightness and darkness, soft and hard, simple and complex, and of easy and difficult, blend into this one word—love. The more we search, the more we realize it is right next to us each day.

I am with you always, until the end of the age. Matthew 28:20

For where two or three are gathered together in My name, I am there in the midst of them. Matthew 18:20

I will never leave you nor forsake you. Hebrews 13:5

Greater love has no one than this, than to lay down one's life for his friends. John 15:13

So simple to say, yet difficult to believe. Difficult to believe yet simple to have. Understand love, and understand God. Light is your key to realizing the treasure of life. It is a gift from our Creator to show you His love through truth. Exercise your heart to keep your mind busy, and *know love well.*

"We can easily forgive a child who is afraid of the dark; the real tragedy of life is when men are afraid of the light."

Plato
(427 – 347 BC)

I Know Love Well Dedication

I dedicate *I Know Love Well* to my second grandson Adam David Engle. Before you were born, I loved you. Before you were with us to hold and caress, kiss and watch at play, you were loved by many people. You were conceived in love and my wish for you is that you will experience love and love more than you were loved—even before you were born. To know God is to know love, light, truth and infinity.

I Love You,
Grandpa Bair

By this we know love, because He laid down His life for us. And we also ought to lay down our lives for the brethren.

1 John 3:16

I Know Love Well

I know Love Well.
  It's the boring times made happy,
The rough times all smoothed out.
  Sacrifices willingly accepted,
With pride, old shoes worn thin.

When difficult relationships,
  Fueled by heart, run out.
It's the minutes and the hours,
  Of each day, each week, and year;

Saved up like hickory hardwood,
  Seasoned best for fire.
Slow ember hot and clean,
  Warming chilled emotions.

As faithful as the stars light,
  A dark sky unyielding secrets.
Love asks only commitment for its treasures;
  I know Love well.

Focus Narrative

"You can't depend on your eyes when your imagination is out of focus."   Mark Twain

Focus is a free form verse. I'm writing it to myself mostly, but at the same time I want others to take notice and try to do the same. How often we ponder thoughts and words only to forget them all at crunch time. It is discipline of the heart and mind that prepares us for the daily din of reckless noise and sin competing for our souls.

As the warrior disciplines his aim, the artist repeats her brush strokes; as the musician revisits his scales, the actress rehearses her lines; as the athlete practices his moves, so we need diligent pursuit in excellence of the heart.

Surround yourself with beauty. Sing a pleasant hymn. Voice sweet affection with compliments. More than anything, focus on the truth. Practice, practice, practice.

Awash in fear and doubt, your slumber thoughts will lift you up. In brilliant light of day, truth starts very small in your brain. An angel will smile at you. A child will hug your neck.

I had my granddaughter, Abigail, on my lap showing her a slide show I made for her on the computer. The clips were her baby pictures with some patriotic orchestration playing in the background. She was only two and a half years old, yet to my great reward, she smiled and said in a very grown up voice, "Thank you." Then she kissed my cheek.

I had made that slide show a full year earlier and was using it now to entertain her for a few minutes. But God touched her heart and she touched mine because of it.

God will allow His countenance to comfort your weary heart. That is the time to reach down into your disciplined spirit and lift the banner of your own colors. Wave it high above your head and subdue your pride in mortality. Then your heart will soar with eagles.

Focus Dedication

I dedicate *Focus* to my great grandchildren. Your parents will hear this message directly from me. I wrote this down so you will pass it on to your children and live by it. May God always smile upon you, opening your heart and mind to focus on the task to live by His truth.

Love,
Great Grandpa Jeff

And this I pray, that your love may abound still more in knowledge and all discernment, that you may approve the things that are excellent, that you may be sincere and without offense, till the day of Christ.

Philippians 1: 9&10

Focus

Your best is still inside you.
Quit for Truth, quit for Love,
But never quit for fear.
Focus on what's within you.

There is good and there is evil,
You choose which way to grow.
Time, patience, love and truth, heal.

Forgive yourself and others' transgressions.
Learn from mistakes—don't repeat them.
Focus on purpose and goal.

Ignore noise and confusing activity,
That bombard your spirit constantly.
Focus, Focus, Focus.

In a crowd, you'll be alone.
Alone, a thousand memories will companion you.
Friends will trust and love you.

Focus on the inner purpose,
It will expose the outer goal.
Focus and concentrate!
You will be rewarded.

Treasured Rest Narrative

"With every lost hour, a part of life perishes."
Gottfried Wilhelm Von Leibniz

Treasured Rest is one of my favorites. An early morning walk outside our apartment building on Spangdahlem Air Base, Germany, inspired this poem. Our family lived in what was formerly the attic of a tall, stucco covered structure. We carried everything up and down five flights of stairs, which made for a lot of exercise.

By the time one reached the bottom and stepped out into the cool damp air, a warm heavy breath would break on the breezeless morning atmosphere like steam from a factory. I enjoy the mild humid winters in Southern Germany. It is as though I am visiting a beginning place when I'm there. Somehow the familiar surroundings communicate ancestry.

This particular morning, dew was heavy on the trees as it clung in a stunning array on the delicate leaves of yearling maples planted on the lawn. The leaves had changed from green to the yellow, orange and red of autumn. Droplets of gathering dew hung large and heavy on pointed leafy hooks, like glistening crystal teardrops off fairy tale fingertips. The short tree limbed shapes were full with thousands of plump water droplets hanging at eye level.

They held fast in the windless quiet of the early overcast morning as if to be picked, plucked or harvested for some great treasure or banquet. The water crystals refracted light from our yellow sidewalk lamps like sparkling Christmas candles. A passing car's headlights danced through them like sunlight through pliant gemstones until the rising sun shown through with rainbow brilliance. Then, they were gone.

Creation so enchants my witness sometimes, I can't imagine how people choose to ignore it. The amazing thing is that these kinds of beautiful displays of God's laws of nature happen frequently. Yet, they require special conditions occurring simultaneously. You must be at the right place at the right time to see and witness them before they vanish. I've often thought of God proving his continued presence through events like these inspiring *Treasure Rest.* He reveals Himself in many ways if we stop, look, listen and reflect. It's not the, "smell the roses along the way..." idea. It's deeper than that. One must "Consider the lilies of the field."(Matthew 6:28). These flowers trumpet God's glory for us.

Have you ever tried to make a beautiful creation? Perhaps it was a garment, a decorated cake or fine jewelry. Maybe it was polishing the chrome on a car or motorcycle, building a house, mansion, skyscraper, or maybe attempting a song, picture or poem. Remember, it all comes from creation's ingredients and we are at best alchemists or apothecaries mixing, testing and blending what already exists into something new looking.

Now imagine your task is creating a tree with all the nutrients, soil conditions, and weather patterns that perfect it. You have to consider the reflecting light surfaces, moisture from the air, water surface tension and invisible forces needed to create the hanging jeweled water droplets. All must be perfectly suited for enigmatic gravity to tug at water molecules for a brief moment to form the beautiful sparkling liquid gems.

Do it for the pleasure and wonder of one person in five billion, for a few moments, before erasing the images and converting them into memories.

Take all the mathematics, science, secrets, notions, genius and efforts of all people ever born. Put them into one singular event and still it could not bear the unique bejeweled droplets I observed in nature and perceived as gifts, in the stillness of that warm damp, dim-lit autumn morning.

Oh, He is here all right—look, listen, smell, touch, taste, think and remember we are in His image. Choose to remember often the miracle of creation you once witnessed. Now if it were in your power, would you create the treasure? I would, and create it for my own enjoyment. Yet God creates beauty for our pleasure and for His glory.

Treasured Rest finishes with a scene from another maple tree location my relatives frequent. It's a forested preserve in Central Illinois owned by a local family and passed down through generations. Within the wooded acreage, they host weddings, receptions, play paint ball games, make maple syrup and have two lovely cemeteries. Some of our ancestors already lie there and more family members plan to take final rest among the beautiful maple trees.

When I wrote *Treasured Rest,* my mind crossed expanses of space and time to view our final resting place together. We haven't bought plots yet, but it's only a matter of time.

I don't think we visit cemeteries as often as we should. Long ago, they were among our first city and town parks. We should stop frequently and reflect, meditate and pray.

As a teenager, I organized a cleanup of our church cemetery for my Eagle Scout community project. When the cool, autumn Saturday morning came, to get busy, I was the only one that showed up. Working that entire Fall day raking leaves, picking up fallen branches and resetting tombstones, made me realize the finite nature of man. It was a lovely blisters-on-hands day, which afforded an adolescent not only discipline, but solemn meditation as well.

My project was a failure in leadership, but a triumph in humility. My Scout Leaders felt sorry for me so they awarded the effort with credit for my Eagle Scout Project. Little did they know that the Eagle had already flown. Rising high into a Spirit-filled realm, it entered a place where works serve to remind the servant just who is really in charge of destiny.

In this place, pride fails to sustain a winged ascent. Hugging close to the humble earth, the eagle creates lift, through forces real but unseen, to continue flying into the future even as the final destination presents itself under foot. To this day, I like cemeteries and try to live before I die, before I live again—in the light.

"Although the whole of this life were said to be nothing but a dream and the physical world nothing but a phantasm, I should call this dream or phantasm real enough, if, using reason well, we were never deceived by it."

Gottfried Wilhelm Von Leibniz
(1646-1716)

German Mathematician, Philosopher

Treasured Rest Dedication

I dedicate *Treasured Rest* to the memory of our nation's second President, John Adams. He wrote of similar surroundings and gave me a connection to his heart and mind. We owe John and his wife, Abigail, a debt of gratitude we can scarcely repay. I pray we never forget to sustain what they began, through great sacrifice, until our *Treasured Rest*. I know they are with God.

Your servant,
Jeffrey L. Bair

"Come to Me, all you who labor and are heavy laden and I will give you rest."

Matthew. 11:28

And I said "Oh that I had wings like a dove! For then I would fly away and be at rest."

Psalm 55:6

Treasured Rest

Delicate maple, talon barbs grip,
  Treed treasure trove, wet diamond shards slip.
Each intricate carat, sunbeams bless,
  With crystalline, refracted, gentleness.

At least a million pliant gems cling,
  Tempered to branch, from long limb slow swing.
A thousand hands, dispose dew's embrace,
  Fragile mistlets roll down, leafy flume race.

Tentacle tipped leaves, tickle jewels roan,
  Sudden brisk shock, can steal a king's throne.
Green branch spry spring, yanks shut yawning gate,
  Droplets reform, quicksilver, on plate.

Sure as damp fog, rolls out of the dark,
  Winged seeds, float full, this mapely park.
A wealth, I wish, we always will keep,
  Together, forever; eternal sleep.

Happy Thoughts Narrative

Now for some cotton candy, marshmallow, sweet stuff:
I absolutely love this poem. It sprung forth one day as is. The rhyme, meter and metaphor just flowed easier than the ink on my roller-ball pen. Though the meter is not perfect, I think it runs well.

There was a popular movie a few years ago having as one of its themes, an upset golfer who would often go to his "happy place." Of course, his *happy place* was vulgar and inane to get laughs and sell movie tickets. However, the message wasn't all wrong. Why not create a happy thought and go there often?

I wrote this poem before the movie opened and though it certainly is not a new idea, it reminds me to *lighten up.* By insulating our minds from too liberal a secular worldview, we are able to pray, in peace, and understand our business here on earth. Through the salvation of our Lord Jesus who paid for our sins on an old rugged cross, (He did not deserve) and by His redeeming grace given to us through the Holy Spirit, we draw closer to the perfection our Creator tried to give us in the first place—Eden.

We cannot create this on earth. Oh, God does want us to continue improving our lot. Yet believing in a perfect society, without Jesus, has always been and always will be folly. Without God's laws and principles understood and enforced in our efforts to constantly improve the *more perfect union* we are so blessed to enjoy as our launch pad to worldly happiness, we are doomed to repeat the most heinous crimes, horrible tumult and egregious behavior against humanity.

The signs are all around us. I will not list them here. Make your own list and start praying for a new awakening of Christ centered morals in our population. Then forgive one another our trespasses, be delivered from evil, reject temptation and put on a perpetual smile. Joy is coming! Listen for the music.

That's when your heart will know what your flawed brain can't—joy comes in the morning!

Do you need to have lower blood pressure? Do you worry constantly? Are your relationships souring? Just go to *Happy Thoughts* once in awhile, and smile your burdens away.

"It is the great privilege of poverty to be happy and yet unenvied, secure without a guard, and to obtain from the bounty of nature what the great and wealthy are compelled to procure by the help of art."

Dr. Samuel Johnson
(1709-1784)

English poet, author, critic

Happy Thoughts Dedication

I dedicate *Happy Thoughts* to my first grandchild Abigail Marie Engle. May you visit often and bring your smile with you as you brought me smiles at your birth and everyday after with *Happy Thoughts.* Follow Jesus Christ and you will be better than happy—you will know Joy!

Love,
Grandpa Bair

*He who heeds the word wisely will find good,
and whoever trust in the Lord, happy is he.*

Proverbs 16:20

Happy Thoughts

Fill your mind with memories,
  Triumphs, trifles, tunes.
Crowd out weeds and prickly thorns,
  With colorful balloons.

Rainbow brilliant after thoughts,
  Teal, orange and sky blue.
Do this, and your thoughts will be,
  Good, and so will you.

Pack up all the ugliness,
  Stuff it down the shoot.
To the laundry it will fall,
  Scrubbed down to the root.

Light as air, flakes float back up,
  To pollen flowers where;
Once the thorns of cynic grew,
  Now a rose grows there.

Gather fresh, fragrant, flora,
  Ruby, soft-petal kind.
When you let good memories,
  Fill your fertile mind.

Try Paint a Tree Narrative

Courage like a tall and solid oak tree from a little acorn, stands against storms just as a delicate bloom chances its color and fragrance bravely against a frost covered, blustery winter day.

Author

This verse I worked on at some length, unsure if I wanted it as poetry or prose. So many times in my youth I found tranquility among the trees, meadows, or park grasses. I love a good golf course for its character. I can be somewhere else and meander through each fairway and obstacle in my mind. Yet, the numinous moment of golf awareness only comes on one of those perfect climate days, actually out on the course.

Try Paint a Tree has nothing to do with golf, but it does try to explain a similar emotion and frustration resulting from discipline and practicing God's requirement of dominion over the earth. I believe golf suggests a strong desire to carry out His plan. That is why we build the beautiful gardens, and play in them the most structured game ever invented by man. The earth is like a strong willed child, always fighting to have its way. We corral some parts for awhile but they always break free again. The terrain is manipulated by man with perpetual resistance by God's laws to grow and sustain plant and animal life; thus frustrating the playing surface as well as the golfer.

If you've ever tried to put the white dimpled ball in a four-and-a-quarter inch hole from nearly two-thirds of a mile away, in five attempts or less, with a small shovel headed club, you understand this notion.

We tinker and plan. We build and rebuild. We improve and reprove with our persistent desire to create things. And some attempts are very impressive, beautiful, clever and functional. Where do you suppose the commonality of human nature to harness earthly elements and create things like gardens, parks, landscapes and golf courses comes from?

Do we need science, philosophy or sociology to tell us we seek to create because the Creator is in us? I say our thinking loses reason sometimes. What we embrace as a unique thought is cleverly disguised suggestive messaging. Learn to realize when your reasoning is being manipulated; or suffer a fools errand. Arriving at this destination is wrought with regret and humiliation—the opposite of victory and joy.

We are not gods! But God is in each one of us. Therefore, enjoy your creativity or someone else's. But remember where creativity came from in the first place.

I don't think chimpanzees could paint the Sistine Chapel as well as Michelangelo Buonarroti (1475-1564). Nor do I believe we should forsake our Creator when we mimic His creativity.

**"Science without religion is lame,
Religion without science is blind."**

**Albert Einstein
(1879 - 1955)**

US (German-born) physicist
Science, Philosophy and Religion:
A Symposium, 1941

Try Paint A Tree Dedication

I dedicate *Try Paint A Tree* to my second granddaughter, Lauren Grace Bair. You were a delight to hold at your birth and a pleasant child to share time with. May you grow in love's presence and share the grace from the Holy Spirit the way you graced me with your arrival in the world.

Love,
Grandpa Bair

You are worthy, O Lord,
to receive glory and honor and power;
for You created all things,
and by Your will they exist and were created.

Revelations 4:11

Try Paint A Tree

Have you ever wondered, why no one successfully,
  Put paint to canvas, to make a tree.
Oh! Sure, many a brush stroke image mock Creation.
  But no one, every leaf and every limb-bark can conceive.

The shear majesty of a million tickling leaves,
  Dancing merrily in the breeze,
Confounds the value of our creativity.
"Hold still," a painter might as well try to paint the air,
  Every blade of grass, all clover-soft, would be as easy to create,
    For all her aggravation spared.

Juggling sketch pad and pencil on her knees,
  All the while squirrels dance on the bark.
Each toe hold changes the surface of the tree,
  "Hold on there," persistent painter scolds.
Small chatterboxes never mind her chide,
  "Oh, mercy there goes another nut," she frets.
Must erase that one from her page.

And limbs so bent as not to tell,
  This crosses which from ripe old age,
Look down upon the helpless lass,
  As patriarch and matriarch of scenery assay.

Now frazzled artist about to quit,
  A little wiser for having been so brave,
Sees God's Hand in all of it;
  No mortal can recreate His gifts.

And her tree just borrowed for awhile now shades,
  Her weary frame, against harmful rays these long days.
A splash of paint here and there, on her nose,
  Cheeks and frock, confirms an image,
Perfected by the Master Artist of our dynamic universe,
  While trying to portrait a tree.

The Beginning Narrative

This is one of my most recent verses, finished before printing *Torchwood Calliope* took place. It began as a study of Genesis and finished as a good way to drop anchor in order to dedicate an important message along the journey.

So much has taken place since I first set out to write this diary in prose, poetry, proverbs and quotes. I've learned a great deal about God's intentions as if a new life evolved, slowly, while preoccupied with making a living.

It is a new beginning for my family and me. I struggled for so long with temporal matters in life, sin, and what I was supposed to be. I needed a fresh start to get to this point of comfort in tribulation. I fought it for so long, while bad habits resulted in high defense posturing.

These earthly defenses are no match for the real battles and enemies of God's Kingdom. WWII American General George S. Patton, Jr. once said, "Fortifications are monuments to the stupidity of man." My defenses were locking me in a secluded world away from God's blessings, which nourish a joyful existence. Evil became real to me and I needed to be delivered from it.

A once popular proposition suggested that if God created everything, then surely He created sin and evil. This faulty logic will trap an innocent mind. Satan works this way to capture our faith away from the King of Heaven and earth. But just as other mysteries of His creation unfold as we mature enough to handle them, this fake reasoning allows for illumination of His purpose through the Light of His blessed Son, Jesus, sent to explain it to us. He said, *"I am the way, the truth and the life. No one comes to the Father except through me. If you had known Me, you would have known my Father also; from now on you know Him and have seen Him."* John 14:6-7

If we can believe that cold does not exist, except for the absence of heat, and darkness does not exist except for the absence of light, then why is it so difficult to believe that sin and evil do not exist except for the absence of God from one's heart and the absence of light in one's life?

God did not have to create what we accept as a pattern of choices to allow evil thoughts, words and deeds to exist. We create sin and evil by accepting what the world has to offer without questioning it. We prefer sin instead of accepting Christ as the embodiment of the Creator on earth and the Light of the world. This has the same effect as closing the door to our hearts and slowly blocking light from our souls.

Darkness is real if no light is present in the world. A cold heart is real only if we shun God from our thoughts, words, deeds and prayers. This is reality 101. The fortress we build around our hearts to shield us from perceived pain, corners us within walls that remain cold and rooms that begin to darken our soul. Open the windows of your heart before it's too late. Take a walk outside your cold, dark place and begin to feel alive in the knowledge of *the way, the truth and the life.*

Great thought and reasoning has persisted to settle a perceived disunity between individual autonomy, predetermination and God's Omniscience. There need not be confusion because God's Omnipotence doesn't equal tyranny. Have you never known your child's mind before they speak? Do you interfere with their choices anyway? Do we lord over every decision they make? Only to our peril! We know God's model for dealing with us because we practice it ourselves— uniquely in His image. Since the beginning, we have been His children.

I want to be portable now. I need to throw off worldly expectations and move about freely. This is my new course— my new prayer. No, I'm not talking about fanciful frivolity or casting caution to the wind. I'm praying for real autonomy to allow freedom of travel, reading, writing, and doing the Lord's work as He intends. I accept toil and trouble much easier now.

My tantrums of despair, quiet much quicker (most of the time). Calm assurance over chaos precedes victory cooling my spirit with renewed opportunity for success. And most of all, I await God's glory as a child yearns for Christmas morning. Victories over evil continue to materialize in ways I never saw before. They are constant, persistent and very real.

Our grandchildren keep arriving on earth, healthy and much loved from all sides of both families who contributed to their heredity. We now have five: Abigail, Lauren, Silas, Adam and Riley. As these new creations on earth begin fresh lives with their parents, we are just as blessed as when our own young family began to grow.

Something just occurred to me, and I need to remember and pass on. Fear not prosperity! Terror can block us from our rightful inheritance. It hovers just above us like a storm cloud dark and wet. Fear rains on our parade of joy and dampens the light of truth, filtering our knowledge of God's blessings through a darkened view of His Creation. Finally, it grips our hearts and instills dread, making even the smallest decision that could free us from bondage, too terrible to handle.

Then, as if caught out in an open field of flowers after a rainstorm, we are soaked to the skin by the downpour of doubt. Yet, what harm was really done? We are wet, standing in a field of beautiful blooms, with only our senses afflicted with temporary discomfort. Creation still stands! Only our countenance is changed. We choose to smile or frown, to laugh or cry, to fight or quit, to live or die. In living for joy comes the Holy Spirit. The Spirit will lift you beyond all man made contrivances that try to ensnare you in a maze of doubt.

Each day provides a new cliché. We consider a trite little, "How's it going today?" with a smile to open brief encounters. The world wants to hear negative or depressing platitudes. It is cynical energy chosen to discourage us. Ultimately, the pessimistic option leads us down a wide path of common disillusionment. If you tell them your Pollyannaish truth, they recoil in fear only to strike back with venomous hatred. But their bite has no venom capable of sickening the antidote of joy, peace, liberty and prosperity.

I practice casting my pearls before believers of light and life, and speak bluntly to most others unless they seek the face of Jesus. This may sound selfish or uncaring, but until you have felt the rattler's bite leaving callous scars in cruel delight, it's difficult to know why one's happy thoughts are best held close to a shielded heart. Pray for those who cannot see past a mere cliché to know that trite is right and throng is wrong. It's best to act wisely with a joyful heart.

"More duality?" you might ask. Why, yes it is. That's the way God created it—in *the beginning*. Like the embryo splits, cells divide. Plants bifurcate, as our own arteries and veins, into greater and lesser branches, starting out as a singular element and dividing over and over again.

Joy is the taproot of our lives. We choose how to distribute it above the surface, one branch at a time. Yet, its opposite nature is only a stem away. Our choices decide which nourishes the brain, heart, body and soul. Cast not your joy onto rocks or poor soil or thorns. Lay it down gently before the Lord like the purest unblemished lamb from your flock of blessings. Hold it close to protect it from harm when entering into battle. Share it abundantly with your closest friends, and nurture your joy with your offspring and spouse.

Like music, poetry resonates what nature craves from a creative spoken word. Shakespeare wrote poetic matter over 400 years ago that still strikes chords deep inside listeners today. Bible verses have played their music to our ears for much longer than that. I wasn't sure why my thoughts had to be expressed in poetry until I realized the gift of spoken expression is important to the LORD. He must like music, lyric and poetry. We are His poems. He spoke and we came into being. We imitate His ways and endure in His Spirit by channeling timbre out, yearning to hear an echo of His voice back. Our words have influence but cannot create life as His did. And yet He lets us produce beautiful offspring! Ergo, His spoken words collect in our universe to fill perceived emptiness with what some call *strings*. Man's quantum mechanics are confused by missing the mere fact that our Creator's active resonance is the "dark matter," or *ether* they seek.

In the beginning, God intended us for perfection. We know He desires us there again. The signs of God's grace and mercy are all around us. Our observation of too bright a sun and so beautiful an autumn day, prove His character through our gladness. Absorb His peace everyday before entering into battle. The battles will become fewer and easier to handle. Your life will be renewed, as it was intended—in the beginning.

"An incessant change of means to attain unalterable ends is always going on; We must take care not to lend these sundry means undue eminence in the Perspective of our minds; for, since the beginning, there has been an unending Cycle of them, and for each its advocates have claimed adoption as the sole solution of successful war."

General George S. Patton, Jr
(1885 - 1945)

American soldier, poet-warrior

The Beginning Dedication

I dedicate *The Beginning* to all non-believers. Conceived and born the same as every other human being, your purpose is to believe in our Creator. He did not abandon you on this planet alone. He exists in a realm your senses cannot comprehend, but our hearts, souls and minds can reason. He will prove His existence to you if you seek Him. He spoke through the prophets, scribes and His Son, Jesus. May you enter the HOW of our universe through your own choosing, but leave the WHY to His Son's interpretation—finding your need of Him sooner rather than later. Remember: a cold heart with sin and a dark life with evil, or a warm heart with God's love and joyful life in the *Light of the World*. It is truly your choice.

Sincerely,
Jeff Bair

*In the Beginning was the Word, and the Word was with
GOD, and the Word was GOD.*

1 John 1:1

*In Him was life, and the life was the light of men.
And the light shines in the darkness, and the darkness
did not comprehend it.*

1 John 1:4-5

The Beginning

In the Beginning, all God's angels shouted,
But there was no one there to hear it.
In the Beginning, darkness was overcome,
But no people were there to cheer it.

Clouds burst forth, and terra firma formed,
Heaved and broke; new horizons separated.
Rainbow colors lit a firmament,
Then God spoke out, and Heaven was created.

Blue water rushed, and pooled to depths,
Only fishes could endure.
From firm dry fertile soil grew seeds,
Trees and ripe fruits, sweet and pure.

Stars took shape, as lesser lights,
And one stayed close enough to shine.
Warm glowing rhythmic cycle,
Celestial clock to tell time by.

Birds flew high, beasts roamed low,
Critters crawled lower.
All earth and animal,
Needed ruling over.

Man was created,
Owning dominion time.
To share with a friend,
God made female sublime.

And they enjoyed
His Love and Trust;
Freedom to choose,
Fair and Just.

They lost faith,
And failed to grow.
Instead, spread,
Pain and sorrow.

We know
Thus,
They made
Us,
In the Beginning.

Miracle Narrative

"There are only two ways to live your life. One as though nothing is a miracle. The other is as though everything is a miracle." Albert Einstein

I had to leave this poem free form. It rhymes some, rambles a lot and says what I think reveals a miracle. Space and time are not in our control. Just ask a quantum mechanics theorist. We may be able to take up space and plan a schedule, but our capabilities to control how and when things take place are puny at best. With this in mind, how then are our prayers answered?

Stop and think about this. Where did your last close call come from? More to the point, how did your last request from God turn out? Remember that you gave up on your own power to succeed! You were at wits end and pleaded with the Spirit to intercede on your behalf. But now everything is normal again. You no longer need the miracle. That's when we must reflect on our initial impulse to ask for a miracle. We need to remember, constantly, our prayers that are answered by the Controller of space and time.

Once convinced that our Creator is in control and no prayer goes unanswered, I became a miracle believer. It is imperative to practice patience, waiting for the next victory. I must admit my weakness during the wait, which is really a journey as God allows us to trace His way of delivering on our prayers. There is no such thing as *a waste of time*. That colloquialism suggests God does not know what He is doing with space, time or us. We get jittery when the world doesn't call us, our services are not needed every waking minute, or our self-worth is being diminished. Yet, our living God knows what is in store for us.

In darkness, we spend our gift of time on earth through incessantly seeking self-gratification. This is by our own choosing, and takes God's Will out of the equation. Looking for pleasure, constantly, never satisfies. It's a self-dug well to contain fear and pride, and drinking from it poisons our hearts to God's truth.

By taking us along for the ride in answering prayers, God shows His power, mind, logic and we owe Him our praise, honor and loyalty. Yet if we slip and fall from grace, He will pick us up, dust us off and allow us a new miracle, if we atone.

Occasionally, God will do the instantaneous healing, visit from an angel, or other quick fix that stories, legends and our traditional understanding of a miracle expects. But I tell you, each minute, day, and life are truly miracles. Go study a little physiology, cosmology, quantum mechanics, meteorology, geology, or any science of our universe. As we find more understanding of it all, tougher questions arise. As we delve deeper into new questions, more secrets surface.

We simulate creation, but can't get it all to work together for the good of mankind. We can continue to search in the Creator's laws, yet here a caution needs to be made. We need to remember our search, called science, is a religion if it delves into the realm of trying to answer the question of *why* something happens. Science cannot be imposed as the only truth or faith. We invented it. It is only a part of knowledge, dealing with facts arranged in an order to explain general laws of the physical or material world as best we perceive them.

Science is really about the *how* of our universe. When we apply science in the *how*, it is very useful in making our everyday lives more productive and enjoyable. It contributes to our joy filled existence. When we use science as a theoretical model to support notions of *why* we were created, it then becomes a religion. Religion is a specific and institutional set of beliefs and practices agreed upon by a group of people or cult. The great American patriot, Benjamin Franklin, under-

Isaacson suggests in his biography, spend much time in theoretical musings.

Old Ben, the printer, made great discoveries through trial and error, observations and applications, which had useful purposes for humanity. He discovered that lightening was controllable and fire could more efficiently heat homes through convection, conduction and radiation. He put two different strength lenses together to make bifocal eyeglasses.

He observed and charted the Atlantic warm ocean currents for enhanced navigation and transportation, as well as built the model for our modern postal system. He invented mellow musical instruments, divined the causes of viral infections as transmittable human to human, and started social clubs for improving society. He also founded the University of Pennsylvania. He was key to inventing a new type of government somewhere between a democracy and republic, so unique, modern nation builders cannot duplicate it. He signed every significant document in the creation of our new nation, and survived into his eighties. His frustration with uncompromising humanism, coaxed the tradition that each session of congress begin with a prayer to Almighty God.

These things survive the test of time. They came from his desire to know the *how* of God's creation. These are not the generalist notions of a would-be usurper of God's intentions.

I contend that there is only one man that knew and honestly told us the *why* of God's ways. He was the opposite of Franklin. He came not to enjoy the discoveries and applications of God's creation but to speak God's *why* into our lives. And we killed Him. But He rose again from the dead. That was the miracle which saved our joy from ending. He gave praise to His heavenly Father before His death and even more so after His resurrection. Jesus showed us *why* we are here: to glorify the Father. It's just that simple! By His stripes we are saved!

God already created all the laws science tries to explain. Yet, truth decays, and people suffer and die if our science is faulty.

The more we ignore truth, the further we slip from the light. It was the *light* which burned brightest in patriots' impassioned hearts during Ben's days. It was the *light* that set us free, and in the *light* is where I wish we always would be.

God is love. He sent His Son to tell us the truth. Truth is light. No figure of speech here! Light is our key to awareness.

"I am the light of the world: he that followeth me shall not walk in darkness, but shall have the light of life." John 8:12

In Einstein's theory of specific relativity (we might have avoided a century of relativism had he gone with his first instinct and called it *invariance*) we realize that all matter is slow moving energy. Energy has a direct correlation with the measured speed of light. When Benjamin Franklin discovered and subsequently showed the world through the lightening rod, that lightening was energy that could be controlled, it helped fuel the Enlightenment Period influence, of God's laws of nature. These laws are woven into the fabric of our Declaration of Independence and Constitutional form of government. As the world we live in cannot survive without light, our way of living cannot survive without certain *"self evident truths..."*

From electrical engineering we learn that Einstein's theories, and later evidence of his speed of light constant, help us derive all our basic measurements of space from the invariant measurement of light bouncing off far distant surfaces like the moon. It is the speed of light constant that allows us to measure our physical universe relative to our perceptions. A common set of magnets display invisible force that may relate space-time dimensional distortion by repelling the past of where an electric charge used to be, and attracting the future of where an electric charge will be. We can perceive magnet-

electric field energy at a point comparative to the observer's space and time.

We distinguish time through the vibrations of atoms. These vibrations have a resonance we measure to keep our most critical technologies in synchronization with one another through an *atomic clock*. Resonance has taken on new meaning as scientists consider the universe is made up of vibrating strands they dub *strings*. These strings are so diminutive, they cannot be perceived by any instrument. Until someone discovers how to test the theory, it remains a plausible idea of what makes up the vast amount of calculated, but undiscovered, matter in our universe. Wiggling little waves?

So how important is light and sound? They are the elemental conditions for everything we perceive. That's why Jesus said I am the *light of life*. His sonorous voice broke the silence of doubt to resonate truth as light, and light as life. This wasn't metaphor. He meant exactly what he said. To be resurrected from the dead required a source of energy we cannot comprehend. 2000 years after He kept the promises He made, we find good reason to believe His words despite our modern appreciation for science and technology. Faith in Him reveals itself more definitive than any other understanding of the universe.

Resonance is so minuscule yet so powerful that it weakens our hardest materials: concrete, metals, polymer coatings, and gemstones crumble with catastrophic effect. In the dictionary we find *son*, is followed by *sonar*, is followed by *song*, is followed by *sonnet*. They all fit together like a resonant sound echoing off the surface of some slow moving energy to enlighten our perception of the world we live in.

Light has many interesting qualities we take for granted like having both wave and particle properties. While teaching high school technology, I came across an activity whereby a simple incandescent flashlight, slightly modified, transmitted a radio signal across our darkened class room onto a photocell hooked to an amplified speaker. Turning on the flashlight, we suddenly heard music from the stereo speaker.

We think we know *how* it works, but *why* does it work? It is a radio wave superimposed on a crude beam of light, warranting no exceptional consideration or measured manipulation like laser or infrared. Yet the light beam is flexible enough to allow the radio wave hitch-hiker to download onto the photon particle stimulated photocell. The photovoltaic device converts the light to a recognizable energy wave source the audio amplifier can use to generate a duplicate radio signal output.

This is only one of many wonderful examples of experimenting with what already exists to stimulate interest in better understanding Creation. Through these special gifts, we come closer to understanding the Creator. It's one big miracle of God's Laws governing our universe. Let us not deify the laws nor our abilities to experiment, observe, blend and copy Creation. Neither should we lord science over religion, or visa versa, since both are manmade and inextricably linked to our understanding and application of God's laws and principles.

We should not slight the fantastic discoveries of science and technology. We are to practice dominion on this good Earth as wise stewards of all nature. And because this challenge is so difficult to bear without sin interfering, we need to remember the miracle of what Jesus did to reconcile us to the Creator. All we have to do is get out of its way; not adore false idols created to rationalize our sciences as superior designs, (like an evolutionary human model that does not hold up to logical scrutiny). We owe it to ourselves, and our posterity, to learn more than motive-driven people can propagandize as truth.

In the Dark Ages, religion persecuted science and technologists that were like Albert Einstein and Benjamin Franklin.

Franklin. Many suffered and died for their beliefs. Today, we are entering a new *dark era* of ignorant abuse of a good and healthy people. Now science is persecuting religion.

Not all scientific theories are correct and not all religions speak to God's true intentions for our purpose here on earth. In this country, we have liberty to choose as God ordained conscience to be—free. It is self-evident through His laws and principles, and reflected in everything we perceive and label as *nature.* Then we are blessed or cursed by our choices.

What will you call your miracle? How will you recognize it? Why bother searching for it? Joy requires us to understand where we came from and why we remain here in order to have life and live it abundantly. Delay in deciding prolongs doubt, stifles all that is good and right, and portends something less than joy—somewhere between heaven and hell.

"The scientist's condition as a sentinel in the modern world, as one who is the first to glimpse the enormous complexity together with the marvelous harmony of reality, makes him a privileged witness of the plausibility of religion, a man capable of showing how the admission of transcendence, far from harming the autonomy and ends of research, rather stimulates it to continually surpass itself in an experience of self-transcendence which reveals the human mystery."

**Pope John Paul II
(1920–2005)**

(birth name: Karol Jozef Wojtyla)
Poland

Miracle Dedication

I dedicate *Miracle* to my daughter-in-law Senja. You entered my life as an Angel to become one with my son. How proud and blessed I am to have my beloved son married to you. May God's blessings be always on your home. May He send His Holy Spirit to you in times of need. May He always look over and guide your decisions as the Good Shepherd guides His sheep.

Love,
Dad Bair

God also bearing witness both with signs and wonders, with various miracles, and gifts of the Holy Spirit, according to His own will.

Hebrews 2:4

Miracle

It only takes one miracle, to teach us right from wrong,
A miracle can be, as simple as a song.
The Grace you get when first you meet,
A welcome Spirit, no object controlling fate.
You analyze the circumstance,
But odds are far too great.

Having said a prayer just now,
Suddenly things change.
Ego and pride are sure it was you,
Yet heart knows abilities too strained.
Time stands still while you respond,
And quickly, without thought, you proceed.

Forces, greater than mind guide you along,
The gauntlet you must pass to succeed.
Then it is done; no time to correct,
And everything turned out well.
This is your soul telling your mind,
The difference in heaven and hell.

Prepare ye the journey now, with knapsack and staff,
Your walk through life is easier, with miracles on your behalf.
You only get the miracle you need;
Don't be fooled to reason why.
When other's stories yield something more grand,
Remember: both great and modest miracles,
Come from God's Hand.

Old Friend Narrative

This poem was a labor of love based on a need to tell my friends how I appreciate them. Friendship is a special gift. It comes infrequently and usually by way of an unlikely event. I have very few friends, yet I long for each man to be my friend.

I challenge them the way I want to be challenged. But today our culture is teaching us to stop testing each other. Call this whatever you like, but I say it is unfriendly.

Remember the golden rule? "Treat others as you wish to be treated."

That doesn't mean you ignore my weakness, I'll ignore yours and then we'll be friends. That's apathy, indifference and acquaintance at best—a mere passing in the fog.

I challenge you right now! Reflect on one person that was nice to you all the time. What is that person's name? How does the memory make you feel? Did you grow in their company? Do you respect, esteem or admire that person?

Now remember the person who challenged your spirit. Not the bully who tortured you, but the one who pushed you beyond your limits; the one who pestered your comfort zone. Think of one who said, "All right, either do it, or shut up!"

What is that person's name? That person was a friend. Maybe it was a teacher, pastor, supervisor, classmate, sibling, parent or your Drill Instructor. Explain that feeling you just had. Isn't it a deeper emotion? Didn't you smile and feel like crying at the same time? While you thought they were a problem, realistically that one person helped you grow.

Do you remember your Military Training Instructor's name? I do, and so does every person I talk to about their Basic Training experience. It was over 30 years ago at Lackland, Air Force Base and my instructor was Sgt Campbell. I remember his smile and his fury. I know there are a fair number of people who remember my name too for when I was their military instructor, teacher, trainer, coach or commander.

If I wanted to have many acquaintances, I could have stayed home and wove connections. Instead, I left home and made real friends. I may never see them on earth again, but I love them all the more for the way they pushed me beyond comfort to find victory.

It's a very special time when a vacation takes us to see and enjoy the company of friends won in hard fought battles. Relationships were tempered in the blast furnace of desperate conditions with spirited mettle hammered and honed by absolute loyalty, trust and honor; quenched by the fountain of pure victory—time tested, without compromise, still razor sharp.

I know friendship and I long to see my dearest friend, Jesus, who not only pushes me everyday to achieve victory over death, sin and evil, but also sacrificed his life that I might live more fully, and abundantly.

"Be courteous to all, but intimate with few, and let those few be well tried before you give them your confidence. True friendship is a plant of slow growth, and must undergo and withstand the shocks of adversity before it is entitled to the appellation."

George Washington
(1732 - 1799)

First President
of The United States of America

First and Best Commander-in-Chief
of American Forces

Old Friend Dedication

I dedicate *Old Friend* to my brother Dave. You were my first friend who acted in a paternal role helping me with big decisions. I appreciate all your advice and for always challenging me to be a man. May you find in God's love all you need to sustain your heart and to follow His principles to find joy and abundant life.

Love,
Jeff

A man who has friends must himself be friendly,
But there is a friend who sticks closer than a brother.

Proverbs 18:24

Old Friend

What is this feeling coming over me?
  Enchanted moment, fading much too fast.
A vision gently rushed for all to see,
  Only my net caught, what memory cast.

Blush tonal emotions, of days gone by,
  Sing melodies sipping strawberry wine.
Induce me to forget an auld lang syne.
  New stranger injects upbraided old lines.

They tried to threaten me today,
  "We'll send your family far away."
"No brag just fact," the old man swayed.
  I wish now, I had always stayed.

Too late you over zealous twit,
  Too late to ponder over it.
Can't stay, must go; before I do,
  Just one thing left to say to you.

"God Bless and Keep you until then,
  I'll be back soon, good-bye old friend."

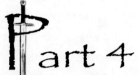

Part 4

Battle Joined

Warrior's Song

These poems arose from years of camaraderie, esprit de corps, hard work, and causes greater than self, in a military brotherhood. I am a husband, parent, coach, commander, teacher, and technician; a troubleshooter, leader and Mentor—trying to pass on my lessons learned to help others avoid mistakes and to share encouragement. All people, including myself, need experience to learn. With the caveat that nature allows learning to hurt sometimes, a warrior's heart sustains injury to achieve victory.

Life would have been easier and more prosperous had I never left home. Yet, when you've danced on the edge of a righteous cause to help set people free, your reward comes during solitary moments, in minted memories cashed to purchase heartfelt satisfaction. My own experiences are more unique than most, but pale in comparison to other's grand times and greater accomplishments. I was privileged to witness virtue in the company of greatness.

The next few pages are my warrior experiences in poetry relating to an airman's life from 1975 to 1994. It began during a period of low national morale due to poor political decisions, entrepreneurial corruption, and cultural moral decay.

In the 1970s, one result of our nation's collective depravity and bad judgment, came from leadership dismantling and destroying national pride for and in our armed forces. Economically and mentally, the nation was in a depression. We needed God to intervene. Americans returned to prayer, and by 1989, it was clear, they were answered.

I enlisted at 17 years of age, ignorant of the larger world around me. Growing up in a small neighborhood where we played war games and fought constantly, impressed the military as a respectable endeavor worthy of my commitment. Besides, it was offering free stuff like college education, health care, and amenities including regular meals, a warm bed, new clothing, shoes, boots, decent money and a retirement.

I vividly remember stepping off the bus from the airport (my first airplane ride), and meeting my M.T.I. Drill Sergeant in the humid shadows between early morning canopy lights. We went straight to the chow hall where brighter lights and a combined odor of wet mops and institutional cooking stung my eyes and nostrils. A tray full of food went down hard with strange, aggravated people yelling at us. A fresh banana seemed a luxury, while regular meals took getting used to.

"Finish two glasses of water before any soda. Eat what you take. Don't waste food. Hurry up! We've got training to do." All the while, *tap! tap! tap!* went their shoes on highly polished tiled floors.

Six years later, I was one of the aggravating men, with a funny round hat, pushing *rainbows* (new recruits) through the chow line. Our nation was out of its sick bed and on the mend. It was 1981 and I remember hearing that we had over 35,000 trainees on base at one time. Today, the Air Force graduates about that number from basic training in a full year! The training hours were never ending because there was no pause in receiving new recruits.

The schedule was packed. We experimented with 100 trainees in a flight (50 was the norm) just to move them through processing and instruction more efficiently. I went a full year without ever graduating a flight, hopping from rainbows to *pickles* (two-week trainees) repeatedly without a day off. Countless times, I went to the shoe repair shop for new leather soles on my worn marching shoes or for rubber on my boots. By miracles, I will not elaborate on here, I finished a Bachelor of Science degree while an M.T.I. Then I applied for and was accepted to the Air Force Officer Training School (OTS). Timing was on my side as Spirit led the way.

I became OTS Squadron Commander of the finest group of people with whom I had the privilege to serve. Competition was tough; yet, my small group set school records as we took every available award. I was blessed to be a *distinguished graduate*, while my family patiently waited for my return.

After OTS, I attended 3 months of nuclear missile launch officer training in California. Then my wife and three children joined me in Rapid City, South Dakota for four years of nuclear missile duty. After missiles, I was itching to get back to Lackland for some basic training leadership experience, but found my plans had been thwarted. We were kept in South Dakota for another year commanding a B-1 Bomber, tanker and a flying command post aircraft Organizational Maintenance Squadron (OMS).

Before officially becoming the 28th OMS Section Commander, I worked in that division while finishing my missile duty commitment. During this time, I worked two jobs, 3 months without a day off. Then, one night, I was invited to walk through the wreckage of a downed B-1 Bomber.

The sight of this powerful machine in pieces smoldering and glowing red in the dark, left me in awe of man's splendid gift for inventiveness, coexisting with his terrible capacity for error. The four-man bomber crew escaped death in the crash. The last member ejected only a couple of seconds before impact. It was a sobering event of trial, failure and triumph that I will never forget. Walking through that bomber wreckage became a lasting memory of failed leadership for me.

Months later, by merely being in the right place at a desperate time, I received the command of this experimental 900 person (larger than most air wings) aircraft maintenance squadron, a few weeks before a major inspection that held the fate of many careers in the balance. Even more daunting was the daily high-level attention and scrutiny this outfit was under because of its unique mission with experimental aircraft that would effect the outcome of world events. We were responsible for the entire flight line, the people, the buildings, the equipment and the aircraft. The bombers and support equipment alone cost the American public around six billion dollars!

I gambled, under the stress of too much responsibility and too few resources, neglecting my primary area of responsibility (administration), and scored only "marginal" in that area. The rest of my responsibilities received "Excellent," and "Outstanding" scores. So with an overall "Excellent" rating in combat equipment preparedness, I was forgiven my file cabinet transgressions. What helped assuage my messy file rating was being able to show the Inspector General, the Soviet Empire and the world, that we could generate formidable air power anytime, to flexibly respond to any aggression, anywhere on the planet. I was a warrior, not a paper pusher. I wouldn't have known the correct filing procedure if it bit me!

I enjoy remembering most from these times, the troops under our charge. We had a practice of visiting the flight line with cold drinks in the hot summer, hot chocolate and cookies in winter, kicking butts and encouraging efforts in between.

My First Sergeants and I rode four wheel ATVs up and down the flight line to talk with our overworked troops. We came down hard on slackers and praised the performers. My command was firm but fair. Everyone got the same treatment. Morale was high because our Colonel worked harder than we did and supported innovation.

I was a young Captain at the time. I retired an old Captain and I loved being a *Captain and Commander.*

Five years was enough in South Dakota. So, I volunteered to take an executive officer job in sunny California. In the middle of a 50-below-zero wind chilled snowstorm, I packed up my family for a trip across the frozen plains and over the Rocky Mountains to ten months of absolute operational heaven.

During this Air Rescue and Air Weather Service duty, I flew in HH-1, HH-3 and Black Hawk helicopters; C-130, air refueling tankers, and converted C-135 special duty aircraft; rubbed elbows with the Air Force Special Operations, Weather, and Intelligence forces, while learning politics from "the big boys."

The helicopter jockeys flew me over the North Central Prairie states nuclear missile fields, doing touch and go maneuvers on top of high pinnacles looking for eagle nests. They took me to the Florida Everglades for crock training, evasive maneuver training and a Space Shuttle Launch Close Air Rescue mission. They flew me in an eye-opening recon mission over the North Korean Demilitarized Zone, with low level landing zone touch and go training. One hasty rice paddy touch down got us below North Korean radar.

Then, somehow in the middle of monitoring a real world downed F-15 pilot rescue mission in Alaska, I found myself in a separate rescue mission pulling Pararescue Troops, civilians and their dogs off the top of Mount Susitna outside of Anchorage. In a *Baby Huey* helicopter hovering with its front skids touching the side of the snow-covered slope and its tail dangling several feet off the surface, we entered dangerous mountain wind currents as the only crew available to save this search party from hypothermia. Our prop wash whipped up a thick whiteout as concern for survivors walking into the rotating blades (inches away from the side of the mountain) kept our anxiety glued to their safety.

The pilot was perfect, and my Colonel a rock of confidence standing at the open sliding door of the helicopter. When he motioned for me to help, I hit the floor hard on my belly and reached down to grab the first PJ (pararescue man), who was climbing on the elevated skids to reach us. Once he was inside the rocking Huey, we broke the iced over shackles off his snow shoes with our fists, helped him remove the large tennis racket looking impediments and then received two dogs through the door.

As the PJs were stripped of their cold weather gear on-board the wobbling Baby Huey, they took over at the door and I helped escort two civilians and their dogs to the rear of the helicopter. No one spoke as our hearts raced and actions braced to beat this physical danger and the quickly setting sun.

I sat down to get out of the way and watched highly skilled rescuers save their remaining comrades. A welcome sigh of relief came over our unscheduled rescue mission team as we slowly descended off the mountain. We touched down safely back at the base just as darkness became an issue.

I was a small part of the process, and probably got in the way more than helped, but I will never forget the expression of that first PJ we helped into the aircraft. He was reaching up to us for a desperate moment in a way I have felt and remembered many times. I know the relief when someone reached down to grab me out of a hopeless situation to pull me into safety. This behavior repeats itself everyday among tried and true heroes. Whether in physical terms or spiritual form, a helping hand extended towards a stranger, sister or brother, is evidence of God's inherited love.

After Rescue Service, I accepted an Air Logistics base-level command position. It was an enjoyable time of tranquility among a wonderful group of people and a brilliant First Sergeant. We were processing many of our troops to go to Saudi Arabia in support of the first Gulf War. I desperately wanted to be with them, but there was no way to deploy under my current position. Little did I know that two years later I would be living next to the place in Khobar Towers that was destroyed by an enemy SCUD missile, where my own troops once ducked for cover.

Instead, I started the *Mail-a-Day* program to my deployed troops. One of the females wrote and told me of the horror of constant SCUD missile warnings. Feeling a bit guilty, I sucked up some normalcy in family affairs. At this time I realized that working on family matters trumped military duty. Still, the thrill of victory and command kept tugging at my conscience for more experience. It continues today as I must focus on the present, glorify God for the past, and pray for future blessings.

After much thought, prayer and discussion with my wife and children, I phoned an OTS friend in headquarters personnel, and committed career suicide. We went to Germany.

Through God's loving rebuke, I made it to Saudi Arabia for four months while my professional existence was rocky at best in an old European fighter wing. That would be my last operational adventure for the Air Force. It was changing very rapidly and I was too, in a different direction.

After discharge from the Air Force for a second time, Becky and I moved our three teenagers and our meager belongings back to where we started from; to reacquaint ourselves and our children with extended family.

It was the right thing to do. But then, following God's plan is always best, even though weary memories tug at our heart strings for one more melody of past performances.

"The poet and the historian differ not by writing in verse or in prose. The work of Herodotus might be put into verse, and it would still be a genus of history, with meter no less than without it. The true difference is that one relates what has happened, the other what may happen. Poetry, is more philosophic and of higher import than history: for poetry tends to express the universal—history the particular."

Aristotle (384 – 322BC)
Student of Plato, Teacher of Alexander the Great

Part 4 Dedication

I dedicate *Part 4* to my mother, Loretta and late father, Manley Bair. Through your advice, I joined the military and picked the right job. This made all the difference in my adult life. May God bless and keep you on earth and in heaven in His loving mercy.

Love,
Jeff

"*He maketh me to lie down in green pastures;*
He leads me beside the still waters.
He restores my soul;
He leads me in the paths of righteousness for
His name's sake.
Yea, though I walk through the valley of death,
I will fear no evil; For you are with me;
Your rod and your staff, they comfort me."

Psalm 23:2-4

Warrior Narrative

"Great spirits have always encountered violent opposition from mediocre minds." Albert Einstein

I wrote this after long deliberation on the meaning and usefulness of a warrior's heart. If we reason a purpose for everything, and God creating us in His image, we look to scripture to tell us what is for His glory and what we choose to be our own. I have always been fascinated with Christ over-turning tables, and clearing the moneychangers from The Temple. He was physically, emotionally and spiritually upset.

It is strongly suggested that He used might to enforce God's law: The Temple is a house of prayer for all the nations; not to be used as a worldly tool for greed. The psalmist reminds us that *wisdom begins with fear of the LORD.* Proverbs 9:10. Jesus proved the poem true by scattering the sinning entrepreneurs away from His Father's holy place.

This is a very good lesson in the proper use of force. Jesus did not become violent for personal gain. He needed to make a strong statement absolutely clear in the minds of those cheating on God's rules. Christ's example echoes passion of physical energy, and undaunted will to preserve the very essence of Creation's purpose. This is unpleasant business. It is the raw nature of His actions that confound our understanding of a perceived mixed message. How could he present the Beatitudes on The Mount and be so confrontational in The Temple? Speak of loving thy neighbor one minute and whipping them the next!

Jesus Christ is a Spirit filled warrior. He is descendant from an intended association with a line of kings including David, who was *after God's own heart.*

David was a fine warrior who responded to God's will through faithfulness. A sinful man, David stayed close to God by relying on Spirit filled wisdom. He prayed constantly for the living God of Israel to help him solve his most vexing problems. David displayed honor over fear, courage over common sense, and sacrifice before personal gain. Yet, he was flawed in the flesh. We needed a more perfect man to show us proper use of force based on faithfully following God's laws and principles while remaining excellent in spirit, blameless of sin and pure in heart.

Once again we look at both sides of Creation. With physicality, we reflect on our image in God a little lower than the angels. Psalm 8:5. Spiritually, we rely on faith in His plan for us, while seeking His forgiveness of our flawed choices. The slime and sublime exist at the same time. Hot and cold, weak and strong, dark and light, love and hate, birth and death; are all examples of creations conditions for us to suffer and enjoy. The pattern is obvious. Yet, that which is simplest is what we often choose to *ignore*. This is the beginning of *ignorance*.

We refuse to accept the faith of a child. Instead, we create our own false reality in adult fashion and call it good. We harden our hearts to the beauty of God's purpose for being, and reinforce the notions the evil-one insinuates as *intelligent* or *common sense*. We, in essence, flee from truth to embrace a one-sided, man-made philosophy that appeases our conscience and glorifies the body. It is the most widely accepted behavior throughout written history. It is safe. It is plain old *common sense* sane.

But when we sleep, our spirit is uneasy and we wake un-rested. When we drift into a daydream or allow a small moment-of-thought to escape our daily routine, doubt quickens and we feel something in life just isn't right. We can either choose to ignore the doubt and continue building the *whys* of our lives to a destructive end; or we can choose to listen and begin to learn the reason we are here, setting free a firestorm of joy—a miraculous, musical intonation on living.

The warrior is an essential element in God's Creation. Warriors for Christ live in a realm of understanding that breaks common sense rules. They suffer greatly at the hands of well meaning pragmatists. This is why Christ promised persecution on earth if we choose to follow him. It has nothing to do with desiring a life of pain and suffering. On the contrary, joy does not have as its goal or purpose to ensnare hapless victims into a kingdom of hurt and torment.

Joy seeks Eden, but realizes hell is real. Death before dying is a valid option. Living until we die in the flesh requires constant vigilance against the danger of falling prey to another person's interpretation of *purposeful living*. We have been given the text book on living. It contains the answers that careless people tend to convolute. Find a scripture-warrior to help guide your next step towards living a joy-filled life. Be cautious in the reality that while a Happy Warrior is a man after God's own heart, he also remains a sinner.

The sinner-warrior combination need not be so difficult to understand, and invites little risk considering. Read about David's life and times in the Old Testament books like Samuel. He was anointed to be King of Israel. As we try to emulate his heir, Jesus the Christ, keep in mind how sinful David was compared to Christ's perfection. They were both poet–warriors. David was an avid psalmist, Jesus an articulate metaphorical speaker. One perfected the legacy of the other.

They are two sides of the same coin. Jesus breaks the mold by being a sinless warrior. That coin can never be cast again. The payment for our salvation has already been made. Our travel expenses to eternal glory are fulfilled as long as we speak His Name, believe His Truth, and most importantly, follow the Holy Spirit that speaks to us in the small-big voice we must obey. Once you accept the Spirit, there is no turning back through denial. Read about Jesus in the New Testament. Study the art of being a good warrior. Strengthen your mind, heart and body for the struggle. Fear not the negative attention your new life will attract. The real battle, as Saint Paul says, is *with powers and principalities of darkness, not of this world.* You are promised great reward for your faith in this endeavor. To avoid the art of war is to choose death. Arise and waken the true nature of your purpose here on Earth. It will not be all bad. The bad is not that powerful. Joy is fuel for love. Love keeps us alive. God is Love. Love is a break-through to living a joy filled life. This is how I became a *Poet Warrior!*

"Kind hearted people might think there was some ingenious way to disarm or defeat an enemy without too much bloodshed and might imagine this the true goal of the art of war. Pleasant as it sounds, this is a fallacy that must be exposed. War is such a dangerous business, that the mistakes which come from kindness are the very worst."

**Carl Von Clausewitz
(1780–1831)**

Prussian General

Book One:
On The Nature of War
<u>On War</u>

Finally, my brethren, be strong in the Lord and in the power of His might. Put on the whole armor of God, that you may be able to stand against the wiles of the devil. For we do not wrestle against flesh and blood, but against principalities, against powers, against the rulers of the darkness of this age, against spiritual hosts of wickedness in the heavenly places.

Therefore take up the whole armor of God, that you may be able to withstand in the evil day, and having done all, to stand.

Stand therefore, having girded your waist with truth, having put on the breastplate of righteousness, and having shod your feet with the preparation of the gospel of peace; above all, taking the shield of faith with which you will be able to quench all the fiery darts of the wicked one. And take the helmet of salvation, and the sword of the Spirit, which is the word of God.

Ephesians 6:10-17

Warrior

Here's an anomaly!
This character stands tall among many,
Essential by all standards, throughout time.
Certainly, a righteous soul as his should,
In high esteem always be held.

Ah, alas, if only this were true,
But his work is carnage.
His deeds revolt a considerate mind;
Most fear the very existence of his heart.

This I know without mental reservation,
And state without purpose of evasion.
These few; these joyful few, stress closer to love,
Forsaking worldly things much easier than others.

They serve at the pleasure of the timid,
To sustain the existence of fools,
And die blessed, and satisfied.

More War Narrative

"A soldier will fight long and hard for a bit of colored ribbon. "
Napoleon Bonaparte

This poem is not a favorite one of mine, but I come back to it often. It suggests an undesirable reason to wage war. Warriors understand that they enjoy war least of all. Yet, they are ready to do their duty for good causes led by good men.

In the early days of war, drums and later entire marching bands, motivated warriors and attracted recruits. These superficial sounds fascinated imaginations, as images do today for modern forms of attracting people to military action. I thoroughly enjoy military bands and especially the drums. They have discerning symbolic tempo. The pounding resonance musters bold action.

I marched hundreds of groups, presented thousands of parading warriors in full military regalia, and evaluated the synchronized performance of once individual characters, who became matched-martial, marching professionals—all to the rhythm of beating drums.

Before an arbitrary disdain for war casts your heart and mind into a compelling edifice of righteous indignation against all forms of battle, consider this. War is conducted offensively, defensively and in our times, to cordon and contain the spread of evil. Entire civilizations disappear when they are ill prepared for war. American warfare is unique in human history. We fight and die to protect a notion that all men are created free and equal. This perturbs would-be tyranny into hostility. We either maintain a moral mighty military, or prepare to live as slaves. With reason, wisdom and courage, we enter into battle rightly, if our cause be just and Spirit filled.

It is a part of our heritage to hold the high ground for humanity to flourish in all loving pursuits, while defending our Creator's requirement to have dominion over earth.

In OTS, we could earn merits by volunteering to do supportive things around the base. My senior flight leaders talked me into playing in the OTS band. I am not a musician, but they needed someone to carry the base drum.

I reluctantly agreed, they smiled, and I found out later why. The drum was heavy and everyone marched in time with the base drumbeat. My tempo skills were lacking and I caught grief for senior students' parades not being up to par.

I thoroughly enjoyed being on stage with the pep-band at auditorium packed events. Our favorite tunes included anything patriotic, the Air Force Song, and the theme from Hogan's Heroes. Though the base drum was heavy, and I often hit my fingers on the rim when playing, I learned to love being the tempo-setter.

Uniformed men and women followed it. If we were marching off to war, I'm sure its beat would have led them into harm's way. I hope that the next time war drums sound, they will be for a righteous cause that no one, but fools and cowards will say the cause wasn't worth the lives lost. May our leaders learn this before ordering the drums of war to begin their heartfelt, influential rhythmic beat.

"Beware the leader who bangs the drums of war in order to whip the citizenry into a patriotic fervor, for patriotism is indeed a double-edged sword. It both emboldens the blood, as it closes the mind."

**Julius Caesar
(100 – 44 BC)**

Emperor of Rome

More War Dedication

I dedicate *More War* to our veterans of all American wars. The drum beats for you as you reasoned a worthy cause to fight for. You followed and did your duty so that others may enjoy freedom, peace and tranquility. You deserve our love and admiration. Well done! May God find you pure of heart and clean as fresh snow through the shed blood of our Savior, Jesus the Christ, on your journey home to Him.

The base drummer,
Cadet Major Bair

Every purpose is established by counsel;
By wise counsel wage war.

Proverbs 20:18

More War

Drum humbly "More War," drum song,
Tum, trum-a-tum, Tum, trum-a-tum, Tum, Tum.

Trill tin horn and pipe, with spirit delight,
Shout "Follow!" and titillate hearts young,
Drum humbly "More War," drum on!

Beat into the air, magnificent care,
Beckon, "Follow! Your country needs you now."
Drum humbly "More War," drum on!

In hasty retreat, feet flee in defeat,
Throng, "Victory!" and we end with a song,
Drum humbly "More War," drum pound!

While generals boast bellicose deeds done,
Young others will lie face down on the ground.
Drum humbly "More War," drum sound.

Tum, trum-a-tum, Tum, trum-a-tum, Tum, Tum.
Tum, trum-a-tum, Tum, trum-a-tum, Tum, Tum.

The Hat Narrative

This poem is one of my favorites, intending to give Military Training Instructors something to remind them of their arduous duty rendered so that others may learn, serve and survive. *The Hat* conveys a need to pass on our lessons and strength of spirit to our sons and daughters.

After leaving the Air Force in 1978, I was enjoying a soft civilian life full of family matters, bowling nights and a cushy job with a high-tech company that had no competition. Even my Air National Guard duty was light, and more party than work. I was bored and not very happy as the world-wide depression swirled around us, threatening our very existence.

So, I applied for a special duty assignment, and was chosen the first alternate, to 10 people selected nation wide, for an experimental expansion of Air Force MTIs (Military Training Instructors) during national crisis. My hopes sagged at the thought of missing the cut by such a slim margin.

Then, one person dropped out and I packed up the family, two cars, and our scant belongings to head off towards Texas and into a new life. God's Hands were in this, but at the time, my pride blinded me from seeing His Will.

What goes on under *The Hat* is fascinating and character building. That's why my son receives my hat in the poem. Above all other symbolic accoutrements worn by Air Force personnel, the MTI Hat is one of the most respected and honored. Even most officers realize its significance and show proper deference. For me to have worn it was honor enough. Yet, I was doubly blessed to be among peers who served during a huge military build up to thwart worldwide tyranny and oppression. Wearing the dark blue, round felt hat was a turning point in my life. It represented discipline, honor and duty—at the time, very challenging duty.

We used it for more than just a shade from the hot burning San Antonio, Texas sun. It became a basket to carry mail to our trainees, storage for notes, pens and paper clips. With a plastic cover, it was a rain shelter. Sometimes, we used it to touch the bill of an airman's green ball cap, as well as touch their hearts—the source of all personal change and learning.

It was said of us that we "pushed troops" as if they were being prepared for some burdensome undertaking. In my experience, we slept less, marched more, and studied harder exerting more energy than our trainees. After a few weeks in training, they understood our motives and sacrifices for their benefit. I always wondered who was really being "pushed," them or us. Many people did not last long in the MTI corps. By the time I successfully finished my three year commitment, there were only two other of our original 10 National Guard and Reservists left in the program.

A good Airman is no accident. He is chiseled in select stone from professional training tools annealed in the fire of trial and error, honed by repetition, discipline and time honored success. These training tools are different from educational modes. Performance and critical evaluation polish human effort into mighty miracles of sharp, capable trainees, who become assets to a waiting and eager operational Air Force unit. A good Airman owes his confidence to the MTI who helped him find purpose in duty and discipline of character.

I loved my troops and they knew it. Over time, I came to realize they would go anywhere and do anything I asked. This was a powerful lesson in human nature. The message became operational as I used power over people for their improvement. Never, is power to be used for personal gain!

Consider examples such as Cincinnatus, Washington, Adams, Lincoln, and Reagan. These men could reach out and seize empires or the entire world. Yet, something kept their ambitions at bay. We are to hold to their splendid models and reach for power and authority, if God intends it for us, only to cultivate His purpose for our presence in His kingdom here on earth. Just remember: it's only ours for a short while to have dominion over, and then pass on a healthy world to our sons and daughters. In this inheritance lies our future reckoning.

I treated my trainees like my own young adult children. They often reciprocated with love and respect. They invited me to their church services where over 1,000 people crowded into a chapel with standing room only. I was led to the front and usually was the only instructor present. After their six weeks of training was over, many would reminisce with me about difficult training days, and they always thanked me. We went through some very interesting times together—me and my 10,000 GIs!

We went out to help conquer an "evil empire," with meager tools and lacking skills. In the process, our abilities were sharpened and nerves stretched to near breaking. Angels came to my aid and one even placed a Silver Coin in my hand to pull me back onto the path. I not only survived, I thrived— broke through clouds of doubt and took a leap of faith. I will never forget the lessons experienced under *The Hat*, and it will not allow me to go back to mediocrity!

"Hold The Cross high so I may see it through the flames."

Saint Joan of Arc
(1412 – 1431)

Maiden Warrior of Orleans, France
(Last words before death by burning at the stake)

The Hat Dedication

I dedicate *The Hat* to my fellow MTIs past, present and future. To my friend Jerry Grenier, who wore the hat with great distinction through the rigors of basic training. Your example had a deep effect on my personal life and influenced me to keep going when I wanted to quit. I give you my hat. For my son, and his sons and all sons and daughters of this warrior's heart, I give you my hat. A father shows no greater love than passing on to his children wisdom of experience, strength of heart and patience of spirit. May God bless you and sustain your flight through life and lift you and yours up on wings like eagles.

No excuses! Get the job done!

Your friend,
Jeff

Have you not known?
Have you not heard?
The everlasting God, the LORD,
The Creator of the ends of the earth,
Neither faints nor is weary.
There is no searching of His understanding.
He gives power to the weak,
And to those who have no might,
He increases strength.
Even the youths shall faint and be weary,
And the young men shall utterly fall,
But those who wait upon the LORD
Shall renew their strength;
They shall mount up with wings like eagles,
They shall run and not be weary,
They shall walk and not faint.

Isaiah 40:28-31

The Hat

Look here Son, a part of my soul,
  This hat, I wore like armor.
Ten thousand troops it did impress,
  And always did, with honor.

Four concaves, soft felt encircle,
  Iron eagle on the front.
While stiff round rim culled discipline,
  From military conduct.

A thousand suns blazed hot on top,
  While warm, salty sweat, soaked in.
Fatigue and doubt, sometimes peered out,
  From below a lowered brim.

When icy sleet, on it did beat,
  Apathy marched quite near it.
Brave hearts made that coward retreat,
  'Round shadow of Great Spirit.

Now place this campaign upon your head,
  Its lessons will make you wise.
Unless it's *Courage,* you need instead,
  Then imagine you hold 'er, and over your shoulder,
Will stand souls of soldiers; Ten Thousand of my G.I.s!

The Squadron Narrative

"Freedom has a taste to those who fight and almost die for it, that the protected shall never know. "   unknown WWII Airman, POW

Squadron level was the perfect organizational echelon to accomplish a mission and interact with people who do the work at a gut level. For a brief time, I commanded one of the largest aircraft maintenance squadrons ever assembled, just before critical events unfolded.

Interim command of the 28th OM Squadron (Ellsworth Air Force Base, South Dakota) in support of B-1B bombers, tankers, Airborne Command and Control aircraft, and the flight line, was like escaping ground effects while flying. After a distance, you know you are sustaining *true flight* from the power of your own engine acting against the age-old notion: *if God wanted men to fly, He would have given them wings.* As a Combat Missile Crew, Squadron, Section and Officer Training Cadet Commander, I used team unity for victory.

Not that long ago, regiments (like squadrons) formed from neighborhoods, states and regions of like-minded people. They were family members and friends in units of 100 to 300, and sometimes up to 1000 men, marching off together into battle.

This poem introduces a very old term I compare to *regimental.* My word is *squadronal.* It aught to catch on to describe the closeness airmen feel as a family of warriors. Today, our National Guard and Reserves best capture squadronal and regimental spirit. We diversify our organizations, yet we don't lose kinship in unit formations.

We worked side-by-side and, with proper leadership, accomplished big things for a cause greater than ourselves. Eventually we departed each other's company more worthy, though heart sick, alive with a value of service to each other, our families and the nation, as our lasting reward—while passing the glory on to God.

The Squadron Dedication

I dedicate *The Squadron* to my friend and 18-month-long Deputy Commander of Lima Launch Control Center, Don Hamlin. Thank you for ministering to me and strengthening our crew. We were the best because you are the best! May God bless and keep you and yours safe, joyous and in His loving care, until next we meet.

Your friend,
Jeff

There is neither Jew nor Greek,
there is neither slave nor free,
there is neither male nor female;
for you are all one in Christ Jesus.

Galatians 3:28

The Squadron

I remembered the Squadron this night last,
  In the quiet hours of my dim lit room.
Emotional net caught what memory cast,
  As mission and squadronal esprit, resumed.

Signature scrawled portraits, haphazardly strewn,
  Told tales of aeronaut people like me.
From tensile strength stock, propellers were hewn,
  Of spirited mettle, spinning too fast to see.

Aircraft midair, happy warriors once flew,
  Operated with precision and care.
None rival the love of yonder wild blue,
  Except for maintainers, who put them there.

Ballistic machines, long missiles in flight,
  Atop an orange-red billowing sea.
"By dawns early light," Mount Rushmore in sight,
  Aggressor beware the will of the Free.

Support for the crew, our most valued gift,
  Ornithic, as Eagle's wings on my wall.
Muscle and blood create air force and lift,
  Sustaining leading edge out of a stall.

The standards I sought, these many long years,
  Tempted, eluded, seduced me away.
Lessons return to champion against fears,
  As routine sojourns begin to decay.
The Squadron, at heart, forever remains;
  The Squadron, forever, remains.

Agincourt Narrative

The battle between good and evil is, according to Saint Paul, *"...against powers and principalities of darkness."* As a utility to help our progress through the recesses of gloom that we find ourselves in or that we sink into through our choices, Paul suggests we, *"Put on the full armor of the LORD..."* This is a metaphor for going to war. It is a clear instruction for bearing the accouterments of being a warrior. It suggests a defensive and, when necessary, offensive posture.

With the armor of the LORD on, we deflect negativisms, hurtful words, and temptations of choice. I find it also makes me a target if I go into the thick deep mud of human activity (like at work, social gatherings, school, on the internet, watching TV, the news, reading popular magazines or books). Our common culture often has us treading the low ground. Who can say they never need such protection, yet appreciate an image of constantly wearing armor?

That is the sinking feeling we get when we give into false logic, hypocritical slander, manipulative behavior, or just plain old bad conduct. We laugh at the dirty joke, agree with a racial slur, condemn a good work, lie, cheat, steal or sling hurtful trash-talk at our neighbor. The armor of the LORD will not keep us out of this mess, just as the French at Agincourt discovered with their armor. Deeper into the muck and mire we sink, until it suffocates, choking us with vile contempt for the very Creator of life, questioning His rules for living, wondering why we put on the armor in the first place. When in truth, we should avoid the mud of low ground.

Isn't it easier to let the enemy think they are winning? Appease their predictable nature with an opportunity to take advantage of them. Draw them into a sense of good will then crush their spirit to resist through promises of prosperity, luxury and pleasure—much better to ensnare the prey than confront an enemy. No! We are called to witness light; love the LORD of radiance—be vassals of truth, justice and mercy.

At Agincourt, King Henry the V had a battered, sick and starving army. They had just laid siege to a fortified city, were infected with dysentery and only wanted to get to the coast of Calais for a welcome retreat back to England. However, 60,000 French forces cut them off. Henry did not want to fight. Yet he could not avoid the conflict.

Consider this the next time you want to run, quit or hide but the enemy won't give you peace. You want to shed the weighty armor and rest your weary mind and heart, recuperating from the last battle. Yet you can't quit, for two reasons.

First, quitting can become a bad habit. It allows the enemy to continue to advance on your happiness. If it's spiritual, you'll turn to instant gratification to douse the thirst of an unquenchable fire burning deep inside. Physical assault by the enemy just plain wears you down until any relief is welcomed, even if you know you'll pay many-times-over for it later. An enemy attacking your mental health will bludgeon all reasoning into a mass of mediocrity that no self-respecting human should endure. All this and more calamity befalls the quitter until a premature death-wish begins to plant itself firmly in your mind. We used to call this, *"walking wounded."*

Secondly, quitting threatens financial stability, educational monograms, and blocks other steps leading to a physical dimension most people in our freedom loving capitalistic society desire, called the *American Dream*. Giving up, threatens our family's prosperity, health, education and arguably our posterity. Property was one of the most contentious issues facing our founding fathers due to its encompassing characteristics of supporting a free and open society. We are born of an earthly parentage that embraces dominion, abides the Giver of prosperity, and celebrates His fruit of all endeavors, gathering more wealth—giving it back to Him.

At Agincourt, the English army was outnumbered 5:1. The French had the advantage in every respect, save one. They lacked leadership to understand the terrain that day. It is critical to know the ground you are fighting on to settle the difference between easy victory and total defeat. Wisdom, courage and serenity were with Henry (also called Harry). He ordered complete quiet and walked through his camp the night before battle to check on and provide much needed rest for his men. Shakespeare suggests that Henry stayed up all night mostly in prayer, and led his troops the next day from the front. He displayed a host of good leadership qualities that have been described as charismatic.

I suggest Harry the King was imbued with the Holy Spirit and he transferred this to his men. The more we try to justify another's victory, the closer we get to fantasy. For who really knows why we accomplish great things that defy reason at the time? Speculation is a luxury—triumph cures all doubt.

King David is a fine example of this kind of leader. Jesus Christ puts his leadership style in the hearts of all those who believe in Him. Other leadership examples, in this book, had the gift of charm which influenced their followers' fantastic success. Most used it for good. Some squandered the gift of authority over people to glorify themselves. History remembers the latter as sorry failures. They forgot the wisdom of Roman oration that reminds, *all glory is fleeting.*

King Henry won a miracle victory October 25th, 1415 (Saint Crispin's Day). The charging French knights (felled by long-range arrows) in their heavy armor, drowned in waste high mud as the narrow field of battle squeezed their massive numbers into trampling one over the other. Horses from each wave fell upon or stomped their fallen riders into the sludge. Isn't this a tragic, yet appropriate, picture of mass humanity following one another to certain and inglorious destruction?

The English chose the ground they would defend, placed their meager forces in a flexible defensive formation and dared the French to attack. The barefoot English archers (with high-tech longbows) and unarmored soldiers, maneuvered in and around the helpless, overly protected French, who were trampled in the mud, too weighted to rise up enough to avoid the crushing mass of their own men rushing, wave after wave into the same helpless situation. This portrays a need to prepare for battle in a different way.

The French soldiers required either enlightened leadership to have made different decisions that day (the leaders also were destroyed by their own poor plan and pride), or they needed a savior—a deliverer from the mess they were in.

They had neither. The French simply swelled war ranks in time to die at the hands of a battered lesser force. For them, there was no second chance. How acceptable is it to allow for such mistakes by bad leadership? What if an entire nation had only one chance to defend itself from an unmerciful enemy and it did not have the right leadership for the war? What if you take off the armor of the LORD just to survive in a popular culture that uses your armor against you? How would your soul survive the onslaught of darkness with all its cleverness and warm subtle twists on natural laws?

Be flexible. Be prepared. Know the Spirit intimately so you can maneuver off the mud-saturated field to a higher and dryer place (like home, church, contemplation room, or new job). Then put on the full armor of the LORD once again and stand your ground. Don't give up one inch—not one step. Brace yourself for the attack of darkness that tries to overshadow your joy. Be prepared to trumpet God's glory. Rally other believers to join with you in the struggle to defend the high ground against all enemies, foreign and domestic.

Advance with the knowledge that forward is often downhill,

giving the charge advantage of momentum, but can lead to a deep mud that will pull you down.

Avoid the bad ground. Seek out a good position that will encourage a strong defense (like a better conversation, friends that put limits on behavior, and places free of sordid images and vulgarity). If you are bombarded by devastating attacks of deliberate guilt, punishing abuse, nonstop torment from people you simply cannot get away from, do this: say, "Dear Heavenly Father cast down my evil enemy that I might be relieved of this burden. Help me LORD. In Jesus' Name I ask for protection from the evil-one and deliverance from this evil force that attacks my heart, threatening to weaken my resolve." Always ask it in Jesus' name to champion your need.

"*Whatever is not from faith is sin,*"Romans 14:23. Whatever is not healing is evil. When David went out to battle the giant Goliath, he refused the armor of the king. He called upon the God of Israel to shield him in the terribly lopsided duel he entered into against a force much larger and better equipped than himself. Like David, you won't always need armor if you call upon the mighty name of the Lord Jesus Christ for help. His Spirit moves even before the words pass from your lips. A host of angels will surround you. They are a presence you will feel, like a base frequency that touches you deeply and a high tone that tickles the skin, your body will radiate strength.

God's energy is all powerful. Calling up the reserves is a flexible tactic that gets results. Like United States Union forces pushing forward July 3rd, 1863, at the Gettysburg Battlefield *Bloody Angle* (the *high water mark* of our nation's desperate battle to correct constitutional flaws bred into our government by well meaning founders who knew better, but were powerless to cancel the evil of human slavery on our own soil), flexible tactics out-maneuver the enemy. I found that armor works to repel known threats, but often, defenseless, lightweight movement wins the battle.

As strange as it sounds, a legitimate tactic exists by pulling the enemy towards you then unleashing great force to destroy it. Jesus Christ used this tactic to draw the enemy away from His friends during His ministry. At His death, He fulfilled a plan to deal with the forces of evil by bearing the entire burden of darkness, (death and destruction on earth) taking it with him when he died. On Resurrection Day, He finalized victory over the enemy by emboldening His followers to continue the fight, with evidence of His power and complete faith in His plan for salvation. When you realize your victory over darkness, sing God's praise. It's real and permanent.

Don't forget a second prayer: Dear Heavenly Father, thank you for my blessings. Forgive me my sins. If I drop my sword or lose my armor in the struggle, please know that it was to call for help. Humbly I beseech Thee, Oh LORD, let not your wrath find me unwilling or unprepared to reenter the battle of earthly struggles. Place before me your wisdom, courage and faith that comes to us through a serene time with your Holy Spirit. That I might renew my strength, taking up the *shield of Faith*, *sword of Spirit* and putting on Your Full Armor protect my heart, mind and body against the forces of evil in the fight. Send a host of angels to encourage my spirit to hold firmly the high ground, while preparing to *charge*. That I may rise up on *wings like eagles* to do Your Will, Oh LORD, in Jesus' Name, I pray—Amen!

"Oh northern mothers, wives and sisters, all unconscious of the hour, would to Heaven that I could bear for you the concentrated woe which is so soon to follow. Would that Christ teach my soul a prayer that would plead to the Father for grace sufficient for you; God pity and strengthen you every one."

Clara Barton
(1821- 1912)
U.S. patent office clerk, Civil War nurse,
Founder First American Red Cross Society

Agincourt Dedication

I dedicate *Agincourt* to Jeffrey Alan Austin, Jr. a friend of skilled labor who selflessly offers his energy and efforts to keep the wheels of economics in our great nation alive and well, and with his industry provides stewardship over his family. May God Bless each day with joy and prosper your works to glorify His name. Best Regards for a job well done and continued success.

Your Friend,
Jeff

I returned and saw under the sun that: The race is not to the swift, Nor the battle to the strong, Nor bread to the wise, Nor riches to men of understanding, Nor favor to men of skill; But time and chance happen to them all.

Ecclesiastes 9:11

*"Non nobis, Domine, non nobis;
Sed nomine tuo da gloriam."*

*(Not to us, Lord, not to us;
But unto Your Name give glory.)*

Psalm 115:1

Agincourt
(Shakespeare's, Henry the V, pre-battle speech)

"If we are mark'd to die, we are enow
To do our country loss; and if to live,
The fewer men, the greater share of honour.
God's will! I pray thee, wish not one man more.

By Jove, I am not covetous for gold,
Nor care I who doth feed upon my cost;
It yearns me not if men my garments wear;
Such outward things dwell not in my desires.

But if it be a sin to covet honour,
I am the most offending soul alive.
No, faith, my coz, wish not a man from England.
God's peace! I would not lose so great an honour
As one man more methinks would share from me
For the best hope I have. O, do not wish one more!

Rather proclaim it, Westmoreland, through my host,
That he which hath no stomach to this fight,
Let him depart; his passport shall be made,
And crowns for convoy put into his purse;
We would not die in that man's company
That fears his fellowship to die with us.

This day is call'd the feast of Crispian.
He that outlives this day, and comes safe home,
Will stand a tip-toe when this day is nam'd,
And rouse him at the name of Crispian.

He that shall live this day, and see old age,
Will yearly on the vigil feast his neighbours,
And say, 'To-morrow is Saint Crispian.'
Then will he strip his sleeve and show his scars,
And say, 'These wounds I had on Crispian's day.'

Old men forget; yet all shall be forgot,
But he'll remember, with advantages,
What feats he did that day. Then shall our names,
Familiar in his mouth as household words–
Harry the King, Bedford and Exeter,
Warwick and Talbot, Salisbury and Gloucester,
Be in their flowing cups freshly rememb'red.

This story shall the good man teach his son;
And Crispin Crispian shall ne'er go by,
From this day to the ending of the world,
But we in it shall be remembered.

We few, we happy few, we band of brothers;
For he today that sheds his blood with me
Shall be my brother; be he ne'er so vile,
This day shall gentle his condition;

And gentlemen in England now-a-bed
Shall think themselves accurs'd they were not here,
And hold their manhoods cheap whiles any speaks
That fought with us upon Saint Crispin's day."

Command Narrative

Learning the uniqueness of martial command responsibilities occurs while working in the civilian community. There seems to be no civilian job quite like a military commander, except for possibly the President of the United States as Commander-In-Chief. No matter how high you go in the civilian world, there are no rules or laws requiring your responsibility for the morale, health and welfare of the people under your control (nor their families) 24 hours a day, 365 days a year.

By the nature of our capitalistic society, a chief executive officer would be way out on a limb catering to the needs of his employees, or even thinking about being their judge and jury. Yet, this is what commanders do everyday. They have extreme control over their subordinates. Because of this, their work is distinctive, and to say the least, interesting and challenging.

The 20th century began with employees receiving higher wages, overtime compensation, paid holidays, housing, retirement and other benefits previously unheard of. These matters are optional in the civilian sector, and those days are quickly coming to an end. I see these amenities for workers slowly fading as a discourse of bygone days for employee compensation continues in the halls of corporate America.

And they are sure of it. We now must compete with the rest of the mass-producing world by squeezing more productivity out of every employee, by increasing working hours and lowering pay and benefit packages. In contrast, a CEO's machinations are rewarded with unbelievable wealth and luxury, pride and prestige, comfort and security—expensed by the marvelous efforts of unrecognized brilliance from below.

A good commander, on the other hand, takes his limited resources given to him through the public trust, and leverages them for the benefit of his troops by innovating, adapting and sacrificing his own comfort. A first-rate commander selflessly pursues the best interests of his people while at the same time accomplishing the mission. He can call upon resources for assistance like Chaplains, professional counselors, educators, the finest trainers in the world, charities, local communities, in-house legal assistance, retired volunteers and of course, the enduring spirit of the corps.

Commanders have at their disposal a finely tuned legal system, separate from civilian law, called the Uniformed Code of Military Justice. They have a world class, non-judicial punishment system for offering rehabilitation to troops and an evaluation, recognition and promotion system second to none.

I observed good and bad commanders and know that life with a good commander is great. This commander sacrifices his personal life to visit sick and injured troops in the hospital or at home. He hand writes or personally drafts letters of condolence to his troops' parents, spouses and children. He is tired-looking most of the time because when a busy day of running the dawn-to-dusk show is over for most others, he still has to shower, and put on a formal tuxedo to attend another graduation party, retirement dinner, funeral or wedding. The best commander is first to enter and last to depart a hostile environment. Equally revealing is the good commander's mastery of day-to-day operations, training, safety, meetings, discipline, and the grind of bureaucracy that makes lesser men comfortable and good men frustrated.

I once worked for a commander who stayed awake for 72 hours to look after his maintenance troops during a major aircraft mishap. He wanted to make sure they were safe from knee-jerk reactionaries and jump-to-conclusionists. As word spread through the ranks that the commander was awake and personally handling the situation, fear evaporated and morale peaked. When the dust literally settled, the silence of official word, rumor and fear finally broke. Unit confidence remained intact. The intense mission once again resumed, in confidence.

This one man's innate ability to lead people in a cause greater than self, unleashed a whirlwind of sacrifice and innovation that crushed the nay-sayers. This commander became one of the finest examples of support leadership, for unequaled air supremacy, that the world has ever seen. Given the gravity of critical events thrust upon a few good people like him at the end of the Cold War, humanity owes them a debt of gratitude.

Our enemies were watching. I can only imagine how demoralized they felt when satellite images and intelligence data confirmed that day-in and day-out they didn't stand a firecrackers chance in heaven of surviving their own first strike, nor match our technology and resolve to fight and win.

It was my distinct honor to have observed the reality of success under fire in many command situations. A written order from the United States Congress with your name on it is no small matter. You become a part of our nation's military history. How much more honor can a person have than to lead troops, in a time of national emergency, as their Commander.

There is no other job like it. No monetary compensation exists for succeeding generations of a commander's posterity to enjoy. No laurels of victory crown his brow. Yet, in his deep parts, the good commander holds a cheerful warrior's heart that will sustain God's own image forever in his countenance, until his final rest takes him to a higher command authority.

To the few who had this opportunity, meeting the challenge with all their heart, mind, physical strength and talents—I salute you. For once, I tasted from the cup of command.

Like a deep dark red Cabernet, it intrigued my palette and intoxicated my spirit to make me a happy warrior. I share your grief for no longer being challenged by a military mission where the finest men, women and materials on earth support the most righteous causes ever approved by God. Thank You Commander!

"I sat there alone on the storied crest, till the sun went down as it did before over the misty hills, and the darkness crept up the slopes, till from all earthly sight I was buried as with those before. But oh, what a radiant companionship rose around, what steadfast ranks of power, what bearing of heroic souls. Oh, the glory that beamed through those nights and days. Nobody will ever know it here! I am sorry most of all for that. The proud young valor that rose above the mortal, and then at last was mortal after all..."

General Joshua Lawrence Chamberlain
(1828 - 1914)
Hero of Little Round Top
The Turning Point of the American Civil War
50th anniversary visit of
The Battle for Little Round Top
Gettysburg, Pennsylvania.

TO LUCASTA, GOING TO THE WARS

Tell me not, Sweet, I am unkind,
That from the nunnery
Of thy chaste breast and quiet mind
To war and arms I fly.

True, a new mistress now I chase,
The first foe in the field;
And with a stronger faith embrace
A sword, a horse, a shield.

Yet this inconstancy is such
As you too shall adore;
I could not love thee, Dear, so much,
Loved I not Honor more.

RICHARD LOVELACE
1618 – 1658 English Poet

Command Dedication

I dedicate *Command* to the late Civil War hero of Little Round Top, Brigadier General Joshua Lawrence Chamberlain. He shows us, through his historical example, enlightened visionary leadership, while commanding a military unit with a one chance, do-or-die mission that helped shape world events. He is a brotherly figure of enormous stature, strength and love. He never quit in battle and followed God's laws and principles in peace. May God keep the memory of this man alive and bless all others who mirror his example of fighting the good fight, to keep men free.

With hope,
Jeff

Second Dedication

To Jay and Lori Lorenzen, for conducting one of the finest leadership seminars anyone could hope for, I dedicate this command tribute. You selflessly share enormous talents and concern for waging God's war to win hearts and minds from the forces of evil. I appreciate your leadership example. May God Bless your efforts as you send the glory to Him and receive prosperity, health, joy and victory in return.

"Left flank, right wheel, forward. Charge!"
Your Servant
Jeff

The Lord command His loving kindness in the daytime,
and in the night His song shall be with me.
A prayer to the God of my life.

Psalm 42:8

Then your light shall break forth like the morning,
Your healing shall spring forth speedily,
And your righteousness shall go before you;
The glory of the LORD shall be your rear guard.

Isaiah 58:8

Command

No greater glory wars receive,
  The man, whom other men perceive,
As judge and jury duty bound,
  Their health, morale and welfare sound.

This chosen one, whom others trust,
  Flawless character honor must.
Nor can he mediocre mind,
  The common sins, he left behind.

A burden, less would criticize,
  Too great a sacrifice for wise.
For by his rule men live or die,
  No earthly goal to measure by.

Nor greater gain by breadth or girth,
  The chance to lead while on this earth.
Greater still to suffer and win,
  The loyalty of other men.

In worthy cause they follow true,
  Knowing well they will die for you.
Because to each this fact remains,
  For them, you'd suffer greater pains.

Trust in God, your path best laid,
  No other compass, this course trade.
When evil thrives on tyranny,
  In its defense don't look for me,
Commanding troops, is where I'll be!

War To Rest Narrative

My orders came through in the winter of 1991. We were to report to Germany for what we would discover later, was our last tour of military duty. I took my family to Bloomington, Illinois for a much needed rest and enrolled my children in local schools for six months. My family stayed in a small, three-bedroom split level house built a few years earlier near the forested city reservoir. It was a welcome respite before embarking on our second European tour of duty.

As God would have it, we were going to the same small NATO air base in Southern Germany that our first assignment took us to in 1976. I had to go to command and control technical training in Biloxi, Mississippi on the way. I drove there in Becky's red 1968 Mustang convertible that I purchased for her 29th birthday. She said it would be her last birthday. I wanted it to be special. Now we celebrate the anniversary of that birthday each year.

It was during this time that I began reading the Bible, fasting and praying in earnest. The separation from my family was very lonely and more difficult this time. I didn't feel as strong a camaraderie with fellow students as before. The atmosphere was methodical and sterile. My heart was searching for the warmth of a burning issue, but there weren't any to embrace and I felt lame. It was in this professional learning environment, with simulators and my final exposure to Air Force systems training, that I wrote *War to Rest*. It was a strange time for American warriors.

I became more at ease with poetry, and for the first time, I read a poem in public. I shared this poem with my military classmates. One female officer said she liked the *left-right-left* association with marching. I was thrilled someone grasped the connection.

Rumors were hot with word from the Southwest Asian Theater that many ranking officers, from all branches of the military, were flying into the region to get quick credit for just being there. They felt they needed the medals and ribbons to pad their military records for promotions. It is very difficult to obtain needed battle ribbons without a hot war, and the Cold War was never recognized as a decoration-worthy accomplishment. Many deserving warriors simply did not obtain ribbons or medals. Others tried to get recognition anyway they could—kind of like salesmen garnering bonus points.

Desert Storm was a quick war won, with the coalition forces redeploying into Saudi Arabia to set up shop for containing an evil dictator within his borders. And for a while, it appeared to some people to be working. Real warriors knew it wouldn't be so easy, and that in time, we would lose our advantage to regain the high ground. The cost of finishing later would be expensive in blood and treasure. By putting off the inevitable conflict for expediency, earning ribbons would then become more prevalent. There's nothing wrong with falling back to regroup. Yet there is something terribly wrong with holding the high ground and handing it over to the enemy.

My poem simply describes a moment in military history that is not unusual—the time between hot wars. I'll leave its moral judgment to you, because I wrote it before hindsight clarified its meaning. Like a paper cut, the quick and clean can fester into a painful infection if left unattended.

Near the end of technical school, I received word through the American Red Cross that my grandmother, Loretta Thoennes, was ill and not expected to live. I received permission to leave school a few days early to attend her funeral. I got into town just in time to dress in semiformal blues, grab Becky and get to the gravesite. This is the same small graveyard I tended as a teenager for my Eagle Scout project.

small graveyard I tended as a teenager for my Eagle Scout project.

Missing my grandmother's church funeral by a couple hours, on a blustery cool overcast morning, I made it to her gravesite service just in time. When I was a child, she cooked and cleaned up after me and dozens of her grandchildren. I went to live with her for a year when things weren't right at my own home. Grandma Thoennes was special to me, and was the last of my surviving grandparents.

The days were melancholy as I prepared to leave ahead of my family for Germany. Looking back, I realize this was a period of introspection and transition.

God had plans for all of us, but I still was not broken. Over time, I realized a new test was being prepared for me. I had to learn humility in order to give glory to our Creator. But it was not going to be forced on me. It was an opportunity to accept the unchangeable and to stand firm—to hold the high ground, giving credit to others and glory to God.

This mundane path was a precursor to the rest of life. Living and working on the edge is exhilarating, even if it's hard work. But living for joy in all facets of life is truly the ultimate rush. This is what the old gospel hymns are saying about joy. That is what Saint Paul was preaching from prison. This is why they crucified our Savior. Just as we suffer from persecution to enjoy the fruits of faithfulness to find God's purpose for our lives, Jesus carried the weight of all sin to The Cross. It just took me longer to believe it. Now I see it and everything makes sense. Imagine the relief of emancipation from slavery (not difficult for an American). Now live it.

The feeling that something just isn't quite right is gone. I know what to do and why I'm doing it now. Living to glorify God is the right mission, and I believe I have the rest of my life to do it! And yes, I would have been more successful on active duty had I embraced God's Laws and Principles sooner.

"I confess after all, that my anticipation of the happiness I should experience upon such a day as this was not realized; I can assure the reader that there was as much sorrow as joy transfused on the occasion. We had lived together as a family of brothers for several years, setting aside some little family squabbles like most other families, had shared with each other the hardships, dangers, and sufferings incident to a soldier's life; and sympathized with each other in trouble and sickness; had assisted in bearing each other's burdens or strove to make them lighter by council and advice; had endeavored to conceal each other's faults or make them appear in as good a light as they would bear. In short, the soldiers, each in his particular circle of acquaintance, were as strict a band of brotherhood as Masons and, I believe, as faithful to each other. And now we were to be, the greater part of us, parted forever, as unconditionally separated as though the grave lay between us. ...Ah! It was a serious time."

Joseph Plumb Martin
(1760 - 1850)
Continental Soldier

On the disbanding of the Continental Army,
June 11, 1783

War To Rest Dedication

I dedicate *War To Rest* to my comrades in Desert Shield and Desert Storm; especially to "Yoda," for sharing your book with me when I was withdrawn from people. You sought me out and shared your possessions and passion for living. May your flight through life be sustained by God's mercy and grace until we meet again.

Your brother in arms,
Captain Jeffrey L. Bair

And you will hear of wars and rumors of wars.
See that you are not troubled;
for all these things must come to pass,
but the end is not yet.

Matthew. 24:6

War To Rest

A metaphor not long ago,
  A war no one once spent.
Medals and ribbons hung deftly on chests,
  Of men and women, who never went.

No lessons were learned, or certainly not heard,
  Because those who did go, have left.
And no one is wrong, they just aren't correct,
  Recounting the war unspent.

Memories unknown open their arms,
  To embrace nobody there.
And I wonder sometimes, if those of us left,
  Are right, to be left, to care.

In the mild afterthought of a metaphor,
  This war, no one once spent.
My only hope is that blood once shed,
  Reason can recall to lament.

Burn Our Flag Narrative

All secondary education should begin with reading the Bible, American Declaration of Independence and United States Constitution; followed by rigorous debate culminating in deep understanding of lineage, heritage, trustworthiness, and suitable forms of thought on spirit; the purpose and governance of person, society and mankind.   Author

This verse sprung up from the argument for a Constitutional amendment protecting a United States Flag from inappropriate burning. I grew up respecting our nation's emblem, studying the proper procedures for displaying, storing and disposing of it. I know what its history is. I understand what each part of it represents and what the three colors mean.

While assigned to nuclear missile duty, helping defend the free world from communist aggression, I broke the rules and risked offending decorum by having a battle worn American Flag tattooed on my upper right arm. I did it out of respect for one of my favorite verses by the late Johnny Cash, "Ragged Old Flag." As it decorates my flesh, The Flag's purpose runs deep in my veins, while my heart soars when it is unfurled.

I salute the American flag, sing to its glory during ceremonies, and have requested it be draped over my coffin. I earned that privilege. Yet, I love what it stands for more than the cloth. *Burn Our Flag* is a tribute to those who first bore the brunt of American liberty. It's written to transcend the need to panic over foolish gestures by others who mean us harm. It warns the perpetrators that something far more serious than offending our Constitution will occur unless they leave alone the Stars and Stripes, which are impressed on the escutcheon of every American's heart.

We could show greater concern for the flag by protecting the institutions and notions designed to insure that it always waves freely—drop the amendment idea, rather be vigilant protecting and defending the Constitution from all enemies foreign and domestic. Let's wake up to the erosion of our freedoms and the undermining of our Constitution by some civil servants, politicians and judges, professors, teachers, pundits and social profits, that desire a different government.

The next time you hear a debate about protecting the flag ask, "What am I doing to protect the Constitution. How am I representing the basis of its foundation, the Declaration of Independence?" When we allow judges to interpret without prudence, legislate without constitutional authority, and overthrow hundreds of years of tradition at whim with impunity, the flag stands for much less than it did before, as another piece of its honorable vestige is ripped off. Let's concern ourselves with inapt internationalism creeping into our courtrooms, classrooms and government offices.

Along with revulsion at the sight of our flag burning under duress, we should bear greater concern for its inevitable demise by leftist school, university and media propaganda. They continue incessantly telling our youth the American way of life is wrong. These people need to find other employment.

As tax-paying, freedom-loving, God-fearing, flag-waving Americans, we need to hire citizens who will cut-off funding university grants, public media outlets, and other flag-hating propagandists. Let's pull the plug on their cash, and eliminate any tax-paid legitimacy sponged from the blood of American warriors represented by the *seven red stripes on Old Glory.*

Let's put more effort into preserving our own good flag by defending the constitutional foundation of the nation for which it stands. So the next time someone burns it, we will be repulsed by the action, because it still stands for FREEDOM!

"Neither you nor Napoleon, could get any good out of an army while such spirit prevails in it, and now beware of rashness. Beware of rashness, but with energy and sleepless vigilance go forward and give us victories."
Abraham Lincoln (1809-1865)
Letter to General of the Army, April 26, 1863

Burn Our Flag Dedication

I dedicate *Burn Our Flag* to my comrades in the VFW, American Legion, POW/MIA clubs, Union Laborers, nonunion Laborers, NRA, all US Veterans, and the Boy Scouts of America. May we all form a more perfect union to remove the real threats to our Flag before the slow undermining of the things for which it stands makes inappropriate burning meaningless. God help us, and May God always Bless the United States of America.

Your servant,
Jeffrey L. Bair

Now the Lord is the Spirit,
and where the Spirit of the Lord is there is liberty.

2 Corinthians 3:17

Burn Our Flag

I saw you burn our flag you fool!
  You might as well spit into the wind,
The good your misguided deed will do.

Go ahead! Stir the blood in young hearts,
  For whom seven stripes were made.
You'll find a hornets nest,
  Would provide you better shade.

Our wise seniors smile a bit, when a big deal we make of it.
  They know Stars and Stripes won't so easily pass.
Why, even the smoke knows a better way to God,
  True inspiration for our Nation's Flag.

So make idle mockery, and burn while you can,
  With great caution, arson, proceed.
For in all human history, only one more perfect symbol lasts,
  Yet the original is no longer seen.

As surely as *The Cross* humbles great men,
  Civilizations crumble and liars rend,
I shall see Old Glory, stir the breeze again.

Part 5

Lessons Learned
Student and Teacher

I shall end it here with three original poems followed by a famous prayer I borrowed. If anything in these pages touches your heart or allows you to ponder life's mysteries any clearer, then I wrote it just for you.

Use it to share ideas and emotions with others. Put your own dedications on the pages and give them away. Write your favorite proverbs or sayings next mine. Then share them with those you love, respect or cherish.

One thing I can absolutely attest to is how powerful the poetry communicated love to the members of my family. When times were tough, I used the inspired verses to touch their hearts and minds. It always worked to our advantage, over selfishness, sin and fear.

Use this book to help you reach out to your loved ones in the powerful Spirit, as God ordained. If you should receive kindness and forgiveness in return, give thanks to Almighty God for His blessings, for that is *why* you are on earth.

We have journeyed a great distance together. You know my heart and my mind. If you agree with what is in print here, then we are connected. Ask yourself, "How can that be?" What is the relationship? I searched a young lifetime to find these answers. I don't search for them anymore—but I still enjoy a fun trip now and then.

Thank you for taking interest in this project. Your support is helping spread the Good News of Jesus Christ, here at home, and around the world. Please pray for my family, our country and me. Pray, and work to keep our country a bastion of liberty with firm reliance on our Almighty Father in Heaven to protect and bless us. Always work to insure, *In God We Trust,* never perishes from this land.

"I pray Heaven to bestow the best of blessings on This House, and all that shall hereafter inhabit it may none but honest and wise men overrule under this roof."

John Adams
(1735 -1826)

Second President
First Vice President
Of The United States of America

(Quote carved in a White House mantle)

Part 5 Dedication
Student and Teacher

I dedicate *Part 5* to all honest and wise people who wish to teach. You know you possess talent enough to provide others a reckoning of purpose, knowledge, skill or spiritual guidance. Go and teach the multitudes! As long as your mind is set on the LORD, your heart is filled with the Holy Spirit, and your practical knowledge affords a gift worth sharing, the world is simply waiting for you to edify. Please get on with it!

Your Friend,
Jeff

Show me Your ways, O Lord;
Teach me Your paths.
Lead me in Your truth and teach me,
For you are the God of my salvation;
On you I wait all the day.

Psalm 25:4

The Student Narrative

"Common sense is the collection of prejudices acquired by age eighteen." Albert Einstein

Our biases are born locally from the raising we had. Family, friends, teachers, coaches, pastors, co-workers, local merchants, librarians, police, magistrates, and acquaintances, provide the human ingredients for forming our opinions. The local weather, geography, type of plants and animals, insects, economy, music, art and architecture help frame our reasoning. I believe common-truth becomes a matter of perception applied with or without consequence inside our neighboring culture. Here is an example of common sense used to discredit a person: *"You don't know what you are talking about."*

Early in life, not knowing what we are talking about is a good thing, (with only a few exceptions). It means we are brainstorming and expecting challenges to our rhetoric. Exclusions to this rule include charting or getting others to follow a bad course. To lead others astray from the proper path to living a joy-filled life is dangerous and immoral. There is no substitute for good directions on the roadmap of life.

However, being silent is wrong, yet safe. No one knows everything they are saying, and staying silent is not wisdom but cowardice. It is a great *common sense* deception. It is good to voice and admit mistakes when learning from them. Stating an opinion in an effort to foster discourse in discovering the truth, even if we don't know exactly what we are talking about, is good sense. Yet straying away from commonly understood lingo (making the local crowd nervous), fearfully repulses the uncommon notion.

Common sense is community sense. Never escaping a group belief or the comfort of acceptance conforms our values to *their way* of thinking. At worst, we deny wisdom, choosing to exist in a realm of popular opinion. This is the basis for bias. Realizing how a community can harm good reasoning does not give license to dissolve our relationships. It confers special vigilance on our behavior through God's rules. Gatherings with friends and family are protected from inappropriate group thinking by invoking the name of the LORD.

"For where two or three are gathered in My Name, I am there in the midst of them." Matthew 18:20.

Try this the next time you are feeling uncomfortable with the behavior or language within one of your close circles of influence, even if it is you who initiates the bad language, false idols or biased truth. Invoke the name of the Holy Spirit, Jesus or God into the conversation and see how quickly the tone turns from *common sense* to uncommon truth.

I do this and then walk away from peers, or acquaintances. It's risky, and exhilarating. Everyone's comfort level is threatened by this practice. I think it is a good shake up. I consider it in keeping with the Lord's lessons to make us feel a part of His universe, instead of trying to create our own.

I believe in being a professional student. *To first fear God,* is the beginning of wisdom. Understanding inquiry, observation, deduction, induction, intuition and using imagination to help us think about our world, are required attributes for practicing dominion according to God's laws and principles.

It's important to realize and practice constant learning as not just a means to a prosperous end, nor as simply an acceptable preoccupation. We are called to pursue God's purpose for our being, through applied knowledge. What good is all the understanding in the universe if we are not using it for God's Glory? How impoverished are we relying solely on common trends to guide our way to prosperity and happiness?

We are all students; even when we pass along information as teachers, trainers, parents, and mentors. It is false and reckless to assume superior knowledge. I was so embarrassed in my youth by Europeans who knew more about my country than I did, that I pursued a Master of Political Science degree just to catch up. Struggling with unawareness of subjects that somehow were passed over in my education makes me responsible for my own ignorance. Like a cake baked with too little riser, we slump to one side, as an icing of bias tries to fill in the broken layer cracks of mistakes, confusion and prejudice. Logical reasoning with faith in God beckons for our attention.

Life long learning is more than a nice cliché. It is commanded by scripture, demanded by nature and so obvious as to embarrass even an unskilled mind. Try to unravel something that confuses you, not something you're interested in. You'll be amazed at how quickly the most difficult subjects become understandable with a little effort. Then, all subjects will interest you and the rut of comfortable common sense will begin to present itself as the trap it truly is.

Use this axiom when delving into research: If the title is interesting, it's probably entertainment. If it sounds boring but worthy of knowing, it's most likely needed and will enrich my understanding of God's purpose for my life.

Practice is part of His perfect plan for us. Discipline is *not* a four-letter word, and is a dish best served cold on ourselves. Knowledge is power. Power aids in victory. Victory is the key to joy! Joy unlocks Great Spirit. The Spirit is our physical bridge with God. I believe this is why Jesus explained:

"Therefore I say to you, every sin and blasphemy will be forgiven men, but the blasphemy against the Spirit will not be forgiven men. Anyone who speaks a word against the Son of Man, it will be forgiven him; but whoever speaks against the Holy Spirit, it will not be forgiven him, either in this age or in the age to come." Matthew 12:31-32

This unforgivable sin is crucial to understanding our Creator. The student must first learn his or her place in the Kingdom of God. I think this is why our earliest schools and colleges required an understanding of scripture. Adolescents had to know the ancient languages of Greek and Latin before they could attend college. What exactly are our educational goals for students today? What reason have they to learn anything beyond common culture one can pick up on the streets, at parties or on the internet? We are failing the basic premise of youth by encouraging ignorance of fundamental laws of reasoning, as they exist in nature, to glorify God through faith.

It's time to reinvest in professional students. Our educational system does not address the dynamic nature of learning. We need to assess our children from their earliest years and learn what gift God gave them in order for them to follow a clear path for learning, knowledge and applied skills. The *common sense* lecture must give way to the old virtuous study of God's Laws and Principles. These are our educational roots. We will return to these in times of trouble, and collective awakening to the real source of intellectual freedom upon which The United States of America was founded—the Gospel of Jesus Christ, and the Old Testament through liberty of thought.

I believe if we discover God's intended purpose for each of our children with their joy and discipline, applied skills and knowledge, will glorify God as He is the true inspiration of all we hold dear and the protector we should trust.

In God We Trust is more than a nice saying printed on currency. The sense of it, is its real value. The surety of its exchange is a tangible symbol of the richness of God's Love for an obedient people. Our capitalistic incentives for success have meaning as we return His blessings through our praise, works and tithes. Then our children will produce good fruit and become life long students, in the most blessed nation on earth.

"A true account of the actual is the rarest poetry, for common sense always takes a hasty and superficial view."
Henry David Thoreau, (1817-1862)
American philosopher, naturalist

The Student Dedication

I dedicate *The Student* to Jason Feddern, a good friend and colleague. May God bless your life with knowledge and understanding so that you can pass these riches onto your children and grandchildren. I pray for you peace and prosperity.

Your Friend,
Jeff

The fear of the LORD is the beginning of knowledge,
But fools despise wisdom and instruction.

Proverbs 1:5

The Student

Always learning; ever harnessing,
Incessant need to acquire,
Knowledge, skill and parsimony.

Ever edified; always searching,
Inquiry linked to modality,
In quest of reason, love and generosity.

Always thinking; ever testing,
Observing finite and infinite,
Simplifying, complicated modesty.

Ever reaching; always persistent,
Empirically gathering intuition,
Pursuing influence, action taken confidently.

Ageless fervor; frequent endeavor,
Searching for the *Great Why*,
Always wondering, yet discovering,
On the day we die.

The Teacher Narrative

"It is the supreme art of the teacher to awaken joy in creative expression and knowledge." Albert Einstein

I became a vocational education teacher in a rural high school after active military duty. I had no formal teaching certificate, almost no pedagogic experience and no idea what to expect. Yet God placed me in a classroom through one of His quick miracles.

During my first few weeks of military retirement, I was browsing the local classified ads for a home to buy when I glanced at the jobs. I admit noticing the teaching position, but it was the furthest thing from my to-do list because I was in the process of buying a local business. Besides, I walked out halfway through a "Troops to Teachers" informational meeting, while we were still in Germany. I could not believe anyone would do all the work and put up with such exploitation from children, parents and the public for $22,000 to $24,000 a year.

I nonchalantly ignored the high school teaching position, wrote down the address of the home for sale, and drove out into the countryside to check on a community in which we could settle. I drove through the little village, glanced at the house, and left discouraged, heading back to our temporary home. My daughter, Vanessa, had an orthodontics appointment and I wanted to be there to help with decisions. It was an important appointment.

As I reached the intersection to get back onto the main highway, I had to reconsider my travel options prompted by morning coffee I had just finished. Turning left took me back the way I came. Turning right would lead me to the nearest town and a public restroom. I had some time and knew that a small detour would fit in my schedule. I turned right.

Entering a town of 1,800 inhabitants, I passed by an old corner gas station that looked small and scruffy. I turned down the next side street to circle around and come back to it, but on that street was a large governmental building tucked back into a cozy neighborhood. My curiosity drew me towards it, while fate will witness it the high school in the jobs ad.

I pulled into the empty parking lot, grabbed my blue cloth briefcase (bought in Korea during an Air Rescue trip) as cover, and entered an unlocked door to search for a restroom. My bladder was hurting and my daughter's appointment time was nearing, as I concentrated on getting in and out quickly.

I entered a large foyer and saw the gymnasium doors in front of me. The restrooms had to be nearby. Looking to the left, I saw nothing but a long hallway flanked by endless lockers. Looking right, I saw a pile of porcelain fixtures: sinks and toilets outside two rest rooms with the doors wide open.

I turned quickly from the obvious lack of usable facilities and headed for the front door to beat a retreat for love of family and relief of bladder. Suddenly, a man of some years stepped out of a side door and into my path.

"May I help you?" he inquired.

With briefcase in hand and cover story ready I blurted out, "I'm here for information on the advertised teaching position."

Expecting a brief exchange and a quick dismissal, I couldn't believe his next words. He suggested in a friendly tone that I follow him. We went a short distance, turned and went down a wide staircase to a lower level in the building, following a labyrinthine path to a dungeon-like, old shop and classroom. Finally, he led me into an aged closet, smelling of dust and mildew, converted into a cramped office.

Along the way, the man chatted, introduced himself and made me feel welcome. In the office, he sat down in the only chair in the room, an orange square back broken, leaning, thing that barely held him up. There were boxes and old text books stacked with years of collected junk and disorganization all around us.

He placed his face in his hands, propped up by elbows on his knees, and said through his fingers, "I don't know what I would do if you had not shown up." I was moved by his words and the emotion breaking in his voice.

It was two weeks before school started. The rest is a piece of unforgettable personal history. Once again, someone's desperation afforded me an opportunity to serve in a leadership position for a lot of family sacrifice and little compensation. I had no idea of what I was getting into, but there was great potential for a victory here. First, the impossible needed done.

Illinois has one of the most heavily regulated primary and secondary teaching certificate requirements in the country. After several appointments at the state board of education failed to produce results, I took my case for teaching school to Governor, Jim Edgar. His staff professionally dealt with the issue and within two weeks, after I was already in the classroom, the regional superintendent personally drove to the capital and picked up my teaching certificate. I was now an Industrial Arts teacher via political appointment, based on my experience, education and their need.

The classroom and shop were a disaster. My students and I had waiting for us years of neglect, filth, and damage. I had no lesson plans, no formal training, and no idea what to do while my students' patience quickly ran out.

Later, I discovered the entire Industrial Arts program was to be eliminated from the course schedule if the principal (the gentleman who greeted me) did not find a teacher.

The restrooms, outside the gymnasium (located above my classroom), were dismantled because someone had broken into the school over summer holiday and opened fire hoses to flood the school. The administration already had their hands full when their Industrial Technology teacher quit for a more lucrative position in a brand new school up north, in a well-funded community. He left this little run down rural school a few weeks before the next term was to start.

For the next six years, I did what I could to hone my skills. I studied teaching methods at a local university; job shadowed local industrial professionals; worked up budgets and ordered new equipment, software, text books and supplies; wrote dozens of lesson plans; designed and built labs; entered regional and state competitions; and volunteered to train teachers for the state.

With the help of my students, I built a vocational education program that was modeled by the technology department of our state teachers' university. This is the same local university, which controls Illinois teaching certification requirements. The same university that would not allow me to teach when it was within their power to grant a nontraditional endorsement for the little rural school's needs.

When I left teaching, the technology facility had greatly improved. There was a new coat of paint; a new egress hallway for student, staff and public safety; new flooring and furniture; new networked computers with a teacher-dedicated terminal; newer and reconditioned lab equipment, and a budget 7 times larger than when I arrived.

We won a statewide university engineering sponsored event, competed with NASA engineers in an autonomous robot competition, and placed skilled students with local and national employers. We worked together to create fund-raising pamphlets for athletics, created our own cash flow for incentives, supplies and instilled pride in our program.

I worked very closely with job recruiters, post-secondary technical school recruiters, and of course, the Air Force and other branch military recruiters. I brought them into my classroom on a regular basis to inform my students of their job and learning options after high school.

There weren't any more floods and very little damage to the facilities as the students and parents began to take ownership of their school. The young adults were having fun learning while submitting to added discipline.

God put me in that school. I learned more from the experience than anyone else did, and He let me know, without a doubt, when it was time to leave.

It was the toughest job I ever had, with the lowest material compensation I ever received for a professional position. These put great strain, and sacrifice on my family. Yet, what a wealth of knowledge, observation and experience God allowed us to have! Becky and my children permitted me one more battle, as they joined in the fight. I could not have done it without their love, support, labor, and encouragement. This was a team effort. We were God's education warriors.

Ironically, the name of the little town is Eureka. It hosts Ronald Reagan's alma mater. The circumferential tide of God's plans for us is dizzying when submission to His mission leads us back to familiar surroundings. But calm recognition of His reasons become easy to digest in our minds when hindsight illuminates the entire path giving clarity to its meaning. Reason, without faith, is notion without purpose.

"It is a profound erroneous truism, repeated by all copybooks and by eminent people when they are making speeches, that we should cultivate the habit of thinking of what we are doing. The precise opposite is the case. Civilization advances by extending the number of important operations which we can perform without thinking about them. Operations of thought are like cavalry charges in a battle—they are strictly limited in number, they require fresh horses, and must only be made at decisive moments."

Alfred North Whitehead (1861-1947)
British mathematician, logician and philosopher

The Teacher Dedication

I dedicate *The Teacher* to all my brothers and sisters in the fields of primary and secondary education. Count on the Holy Spirit to lift your heart and ask God to grant you wisdom, courage, and serenity when dealing with children, parents and the administration. Pace yourself to avoid burnout, but not at the expense of your desire to inculcate reason, learning and thinking into your students. Always give God the credit for your successes and let your students know it too. Without God in our pronouncements, the words are easily dismissed as small personal opinions.

May God instill in you the habit of truth-telling despite fear, and help you to reject course common culture in discourse with your students.

With special consideration for the late Wendy Miles, Eureka, Illinois High School biology teacher who loved students and teaching—the tree still stands!

May God hold you in His Loving embrace until we meet again.

Your Fellow Teacher,
Jeff Bair

"Teaching them to observe all things that I have commanded you; and lo I am with you always, even to the end of the age."
Amen.

Matthew 28:20

The Teacher

I did not come here to barter for your reason,
I came to share my experiences from another season.
I did not come to offer blame, nor criticize old sages,
I came to share my understanding of lessons from the ages.

I came here to spend time with you,
To reach and grow, not shrink.
So one-day you will love to learn,
And dream on how to think.

I never came to teach you,
I'm here to learn from you.
I came to clarify a notion,
That only you, can teach you.

Now as my time draws near,
To leave you and move on.
I feel a little part of me,
Dying and is gone.

At training, I'm a wizard,
At learning I'll never end.
At teaching I was only as good,
As my desire to learn would lend.

Reality Narrative

We have a need for constancy in our lives. Too much change evokes uneasiness, stress, and fear. To overcome these weaknesses, we feed the compelling desire for equilibrium with rationalized reality. Just as *common sense* can be a snare for preoccupied minds, a consensus opinion of realism will allow an artificial cocoon to encourage an unwitting character to disregard spiritual reality outside its comfort zone.

It is often observable to find someone creating a false certainty that suits them, but runs counter to God's laws and principles. Sureness in behavior and choices made, within the parameters of such a loose and shallow existence, always ends in predictable failure, sadness, and disgrace. Infidelity, betrayal, worry, sin and an overarching desire to maintain a base lifestyle are examples of personally contrived realities.

Instead, God gave us our physical bodies, thought and emotions to experience His creation and recognize His sovereignty over all of it. Through excess stimulation we lose touch with His actuality even though the signs of it are without question and easy to perceive. A deaf and blind person can feel the resonance of vocal chords or the warmth of sunshine. Sound and light have a curious reality that our Creator allows us to experience even when senses are muted. *Adaptability does not equal progress.* Our progression began with a Creator who gave us emotions to tell us when things are not going right, and reason to recognize and honor His glory.

Imagination *is* spirit and an important link to our Creator's love and presence. It opens a portal to His Being as long as we have training, discipline and believe a truth beyond mere physicality exists. In the end we all leave the mortal condition behind for a new beginning. God proved this through His earthly Son, Jesus. All we have to do is embrace His legitimacy.

It is easier to conform to current cultural doctrine on what is real and what is not. This is a ubiquitous and devastating setup towards failure. It also impedes liberty and freedom.

Safely we follow the herd, until something separates us from the rest of them. Alone or together in a much smaller group, we enter into a confusion, unsteady, without meaning or direction. Darkness gains control of us through fear.

Like our high school years, we learn to adapt. The monolithic administration kept us on track with rules, schedules, curricula, and guidance. None of it was necessarily truth, but it was an institutional reality giving aid and comfort to our undisciplined hearts, minds and bodies. Grades, awards, sports, clubs, field trips, lunch, disciplinary actions, instruction and advice from teachers made high school an actuality.

Another reality existed in the way we were treated by other students. It was a sub-culture to the entire high school experience. Some people wish they never left this environment, some are glad it's over; still others could take it or leave it. A memory can be a powerful vivid reality trapping its remote viewer in lethargy of mind rather than guiding light of reason.

In college, the same type of multi-layered cultural cake is on the menu—just a different flavor with icing whipped much higher and puffed full of air. We can relate the same cocoon model in all our organized ventures including: the military, employment, fraternal clubs, churches, volunteer organizations, or political parties. Yet, group diversity is important to individual liberty and conscience, through no one entity or establishment having too much influence, power or control.

What is Real? What is constant? What can we rely upon?

First, what is real? Some would argue, "Nothing is real." Others say, "If I can touch it, taste it, see it, smell it, hear it or think it—*it* is real. Let's call the first group *Psychos* and the second, *Sensibles.*

Sensibles construct all reality from sensory perception, and then wrap their *real world* in a dazzling bouquet of flowering thoughts. The Psychos have already thought about sensory perception (taste, touch, sight, smell and hearing) and conclude that a deaf, blind, quadriplegic (with a cold) floating in a tank of warm liquid could sense no reality. Therefore, nothing is real. How could either argument explain what *is* real?

Mr. Einstein's idea of constants, provides a peek at what is more real than *common sense, group consensus, sensory perception,* or reason based on these in whole or in part. He discovered that time is not a constant. The Psychos are correct stating our sensory perceptions can be deceived and change due to old age and perhaps injury. Drugs, alcohol, floating to eliminate tactility, lack of sleep, dehydration, starvation and other things affect our mind to allow for false sensations.

People once thought the universe revolved around the earth because human senses could not detect the earth's movement. The eminent physicist and astronomer Galileo Galilee (1564-1642) was put under house arrest in his old age (saving him from death or imprisonment), for suggesting the earth revolves around the sun.

Knowing (like the Sensibles) our thinking can be controlled or manipulated away from truth through common sense, betrayal, lies, repetition of messages, insinuations, pandering ignorance to affect an outcome, and embracing an uninformed cliché like, "Perception=Reality," can get people to do what you want, but it won't impart reality. You might make *the sale,* be *elected,* get *promoted* or even be highly respected, but practicing these false realities slowly builds a sturdy prison from which many people never escape. Their personal desires spiral into a living death, balanced on lies and pretense.

I mention Albert Einstein frequently in this book. He is at once enigmatic and compelling. Walter Isaacson's biography, <u>Einstein: His Life and Universe</u>, explains how he used brilliant thought experiments to explain *how* things work, yet could also be infected by false humanistic realities.

The twentieth century owes its greatest technologies and modern scientific methods to Einstein and his peers. He began to unraveled many of God's mysteries of *how* the universe works. Yet he never came close to *why* it all works together.

For there was a thief in the pantry of his thinking. His blatant delusion of moral reasoning contrasts sadly with pure scientific logic. It steals away from an otherwise interesting character, ruefully exposing fear, robed in the glory of popular personage, (not so cleverly disguised, and never so deep as to alienate *good reason* from seeing God's reflection in creation's mirror). An epic quest in his math and science persists today, while his philosophy of debauch human behavior diminishes.

Albert refused to believe in a living God. From Isaacson's poignant profile, it is clear that Einstein preferred a humanistic lust for life to a more honest, God serving, joy filled life. He knew the scriptures. He studied all forms of reasoning creation and reality in such thought provoking ways as to confound our average minds.

Yet, he was stuck when it came to playing god. "It makes no sense to speak of reality that is independent of our observations and measurements," he spoke while confronting newly discovered quantum mechanics, which held that small particles (light in particular) did not behave the way his theory of relativity worked for planets and the cosmos. Later, he had to capitulate to evidence showing, "There is an underlying reality that exists independently of our observations." Ironically, the fusion of twentieth century science and philosophy began as a misnomer of his original intent to explain reality.

Einstein's *relativity* was nearly titled *invariance* because it actually describes a new constant in our perception of reality, (light vs. Newton's time-constant). The world embraced *relativism* in morality, by perverting his *relativity* with an occult frenzy that persists today. **The age of relativism is undone!** It was a faddish idea men used to harness a demigod, riding his coat tails into pleasure-filled lives full of pride.

Albert discovered a glimpse into spirituality. The shock of it gripped his mortality so firmly as to force disdain for the very reasoning model that set him apart from the rest of the world. His dialectic consonance (logical argument for harmony) gave way to cathartic dissonance (spewing invigorating discord).

He chose to analyze faith, like an adult, and live like an adolescent. By his celebrity, the wide audience of mass appeal prodded his reversal of God's principles. The world persisted in seeking his opinion about God, which he struggled to know while explaining divinity. Sardonically, he gained strength in cultural authority as his morality weakened.

Einstein's example seems too enormous for us to compare to our own struggle. Yet, we can share *relative* to the *invariance* of God's laws and principles, the understanding Albert would not accept: *reality* is faith in God. Spirit, like light, is constant.

Relativity and invariance exist at the same time. To choose one over the other, suggests a fool's errand. With the faith of a child, and adult dominion, we live God's intended purpose.

We can no longer hide reality. God's laws and principles prevail over Einstein, and all of us. Albert merely discovered light as truth. Didn't Jesus tell us that 2000 years ago?

I am the light of the world. He who follows Me shall not walk in darkness, but have the light of life. John 8:12.

Even Albert revered the Name of Jesus Christ. "I am a Jew, but I am enthralled by the luminous figure of the Nazarene. No one can read the Gospels without feeling the actual presence of Jesus. His personality pulsates in every word. No myth is filled with such life." (Albert Einstein interview at age 50).

So if we cannot trust time, our senses or minds; if the crowd will mislead our path to joy. What are we to believe, base life on, or hold up as our banner of reality in the battle of living?

I want you to clench a fist (you may need to use both hands). Imagine you are holding the beautiful sword depicted on the front cover of this book. It represents the *Word of God*. Close your eyes. Did you see it gleaming in a bright new light reflecting radiance? Test its edge with an imaginary finger. Don't cut yourself! It is sharp!

Did it resonate a lovely metallic tone when you plunked it with your finger? Does the *Sword of Spirit* have weight or is it light as air? If the requests I just made of you seem a bit awkward, then you have fear in your heart. Fear is the art of failure. It is good to pay attention to sensory fears in order to avoid injury and premature death. Yet, fear of finding your purpose on earth is not good. Faith in God defeats fear.

In Omnia Paratus (In All Things Prepared) is etched into my sword to remind me that God is always faithful to those who abide in Him. Passion for prayer will slay fear and set you free.

Poetry may be our highest form of written expression. Light may be the only measurable constant in our universe. Magnets might show space-time distorting before our very eyes. We, and all our surroundings, might be made of slow moving energy. We touch, see, smell, taste, hear and think from hidden forces to experience life no less real than yesterday's meal, this moment's contemplations, or tomorrow's routine.

I believe everything has purpose as we exist to give it meaning. We are allowed to share in the meaning of God's reflection, as our minds conceive and hearts believe. Reality is carefully advanced upon one step at a time. Its meaning and our purpose, are fused to faith in a Creator who is taking, has taken and will always take care of us, as long as we trust Him, praise His works, and not rest on anything of our own.

"I am enough of an artist to draw freely upon my imagination. Imagination is more important than knowledge. Knowledge is limited. Imagination encircles the world."
Albert Einstein (1879 - 1955)

I rejoice at Your word as one who finds great treasure.
I hate and abhor lying, but I love Your law.
Seven times a day I praise You,
Because of Your righteous judgments.
Great peace have those who love Your law,
And nothing causes them to stumble.
Lord, I hope for your salvation,
And I do Your commandments.
My soul keeps Your testimonies,
And I love them exceedingly.
I keep Your precepts and Your testimonies,
For all my ways are before You.

Psalm 119: 162-168

Reality Dedication

I dedicate *Reality* to all would-be believers in the Lord Jesus Christ. We sometimes slip the rude bonds of earth through false realities. Our excuses are many, the answer but one. Learn to love truth, take up your *Sword of Spirit,* and rely on the passion that first brought you to your knees to honor and love the Lord Jesus, who we know is real and died for us that all things were made new. The *Spirit in the Sword* is the *Word of the LORD.* Into the breach, dear friend—once more, into the breach.

Yours in Christ Jesus,
Jeffrey

Reality

Get real. Don't make a fuss.
  It's a one way ticket on a convoluted bus.
You in! Or are you out?
  We just have to know, to eliminate the doubt.

Get off! This ain't for you.
  You're too idealistic and a trouble making fool.
Yea, right; impoverished cuss.
  Don't want to hear your case, it's right in front of us.

Oh no! We're in a noose.
  We could use a little help now, how about from you?
Hey Look! It's an attack.
  But I'm already gone, and I won't be coming back.

Never late, to make a change.
  Getting started, at first, it may feel a little strange.
What's this? I'm feeling well.
  At this present moment, I'm not living in a hell.

Of course. I left the herd.
  And now my victory lies within the Holy Word.
Gotta go. I found the truth.
  Want to let my light shine, brighter than a movie booth.

Good job! You found *The Way*.
  Now leave a trail behind, they may track again someday.

The Prayer Narrative

The first time I heard this prayer I was a boy in a parochial grade school. It was attributed to the Catholic Saint, Anthony. It seems this *Little Prayer* has been around for a long time. Some suggest it was authored by Dr. Reinhold Niebuhr, professor at the Union Theological Seminary in New York around 1932 as part of a longer prayer. On the other hand, German evangelical pietist Friedrich Christoph Oetinger (1702-1782) receives credit for authorship from a 1964 Paris Herald Tribune article which reads:

"In the rather dreary hall of a converted hotel, overlooking the Rhine at Koblenz, framed by flags of famous Prussian regiments rescued from the Tannenberg memorial, is a tablet inscribed with [The Prayer]..." The plaque was on a wall where modern day troops and company commanders of the new German army were trained, "...in the principles of management and...behavior of the citizen soldier in a democratic state."

Other research suggests a form of the prayer dates back to the Roman Philosopher Boethius (480-524 AD). After the Second World War a North German University professor, Dr. Theodore Wilhelm, had received the prayer from Canadian soldiers and used it in his revival of spiritual life in West Germany. The good professor went by the pseudonym Fredrich Oetinger, the 18th century pietist. But isn't that where we started?

And in England, the prayer was printed beautifully on cards and distributed as, "The General's Prayer," dating it back sometime in the fourteenth century.

The exact origin of the prayer remains cloaked in mystery. It seems each time a researcher states the origin, another comes up with some other source. This intrigues me even more now that I realize I have been chasing this mystical wish for nearly my entire life. It is so simply stated yet asks God for enormous gifts in a succinct manner that suggests understanding of His intentions for the one asking. I believe this shows a very early recognition of philosophy destined to turn mankind back towards God's purpose for creating us—an embrace of Jesus—a reckoning of salvation over sin to glorify Him.

I repeated the seemingly simple prayer for years until I realized how complex it was. Then I began asking God to grant me each element: wisdom, courage and serenity, separately to concentrate on each part by itself, thereby gaining understanding of the whole.

This prayer stretches my reasoning with God's Creation being simple and complex at the same time. Contrast and similarity coexist in all that is around us. Without faith in His plan, we could go stark raving mad or accept ignorance, apathy and indifference as life models. Even worse, we might consider science or some other human concoction as our religion and spiral into a dark dullness that transforms nothing, leaving a shock of doubt to blindside our joy.

Faith in a living God who reveals Himself in everything we can perceive, gives us a compass, a path, a light to direct our lives. There is no other rational way to understand our existence but with patient faith. So, I believe a logical mind can accept no other reasonable way to live, but by God's laws and principles. *It's simple but not easy.*

Faith in God, the Father, is very liberating and allows us to pursue the lovely treasures in living miracles made just to give praise and honor back to Him. He has given us life and choice to give Him glory. He enriches our lives to credit our success to Him. He grants us salvation to accept His forgiveness, and to get on with living a joy-filled life on earth until He calls us home.

A little over 2000 years ago a baby was born in the humblest of conditions, raised a laborer, and served humanity as a selfless teacher with a spirit led warrior's heart. He is the embodiment of the three virtues mentioned in the following prayer. He died a terrible sacrificial death and rose into glory as the most influential and best-loved person in all of recorded history. Without this man, the world would be a very different place, and our country would not exist in its current unprecedented success as the most prosperous, popular and inspiring nation ever conceived by man. He really did make all things new.

Jesus never asked us to burden *His* Cross. We all have our own to carry. It is His *wisdom, courage* and *serenity* that we need in order to live a joy filled life.

"To view through the calm, sedate medium of reason the influence which the establishment now proposed may yet have upon the happiness or misery of millions yet unborn, is an object of such magnitude as absorbs, and in a manner suspends, the operations of human understanding."

James Madison
(1751 - 1836)

Forth President
of the United States of America.

On the American Constitutional Convention

The Prayer Dedication

I dedicate *The Prayer* to my sister-in-law Pamela Hicks. Your love, steadfast courage and dedication to family and friends motivate me to stay the course. May God bless you and your progeny from now until the end of time with happiness, health and prosperity, as He wishes we accept and live by His laws and principles.

Love,
Jeff

The Lord bless you and keep you;
The Lord make His face shine upon you,
and be gracious to you;
The Lord lift up His countenance upon you,
and give you peace.

Numbers 6:24-26

The Prayer

God, grant me *Serenity,*
To accept what I cannot change,
Courage to change what I can, and
Wisdom to know the difference.

AMEN!

Epilogue

"A man must know his destiny...if he does not recognize it, then he is lost. By this I mean, once, twice, or at the very most, three times, fate will reach out and tap a man on the shoulder... If he has the imagination, he will turn around and fate will point out to him what fork in the road he should take. If he has the guts, he will take it." General George S. Patton, Jr

After the attack on the World Trade Center towers September 11, 2001, I was looking for some way to get back into active military duty. I found a program of recall options by the United States Air Force for retired military people to reenter active duty for a period of two years. After careful attention to detail and prayer with my wife, I decided to apply.

The application process was not easy. The human resource people really didn't know what was expected of us since there seemed to be no precedent for recalling retirees to active duty. They were outside their comfort zone. I was required to undergo a rigorous physical examination at a military facility, pass a review board for my records, and submit an application and resume. Most importantly, I had to find an active military unit, with a critical position to fill, willing to accept an unknown human asset in the form of a military retiree.

I continued working at my civilian job and put myself through intense physical training. In my spare time, I ran 2.5 miles each day, dieted to lose 30 pounds and exercised to get into shape for the examination and Air Force standards.

I worked closely with military personnel specialists who, after several months, found a job needing me in battle damage assessment. This was a big obstacle crossed towards acceptance into the program.

I took vacation time off my civilian job, traveled to the nearest Air Force base (about 170 miles away), and checked into a hotel the night before my flight physical was scheduled. I spent the better part of the next day going through tests, screenings and lab work all the while hospital staff members were asking, "What are you doing here?"

Six months had gone by and I passed the physical with flying colors. My records, application, and personal references were accepted by the Air Force personnel center, and after I signed a contract, they sent me a nice congratulatory letter. Shortly after receiving that acceptance letter, I received a full welcome package from my new military unit. I spoke with my new military supervisor who said they really needed help due to mission critical commitments and low staffing.

It was a very exciting time (like 1981) for family, friends and me. I drove back to the nearest air base and purchased new uniforms and footwear. I updated my military ribbons since I was eligible for the new MTI ribbon, and ordered them for dress uniforms. I interviewed on a local radio talk show to explain to the public that I was going to represent military retirees and my community in the fight against terrorism.

Wearing the new uniforms and placing my old rank on them gave me a sense of pride that I hadn't felt in a long time. I worked hard to earn the right to return to active duty and it was truly a miracle to have gotten this far.

At that time, a military ombudsman told me, to report my impending leave of absence to my civilian employer, giving them adequate notice before my departure. New laws were in play, which required me to follow rules for reinstatement to my civilian job once I returned home from active duty. I put our real estate on the market for sale as we planned to move across country.

Then days went by without any written orders to proceed to our destination. All correspondence stopped coming from the

Air Force personnel center. I began an inquiry, and to make a long story short, someone changed their mind and decided not to recall me after all.

My civilian employer was not amused by the ruse. I had to contact several congressmen after months of waiting just to get an official response informing me not to report for duty. By the spring of 2003, I received a letter from a new colonel who replaced the man who signed my reinstatement papers. This was a final notice of no recall.

A senior civil service person working the recall program confided to me that they put a 13 person team together to recall only four retirees. I was not the only one left out in the cold. Some, quit their jobs, sold their homes, and had nothing left after being let down by the deception. When the dust settled, we picked up the pieces of our shattered dreams and glued them back together with the mighty miracles of our merciful and loving Father in Heaven. I put about thirty pounds back on, and we settled in for a big helping of domestic tranquility. New uniforms and ribbons are put away with older war relics as we accept God's plans, instead of our own.

We tend to our personal lives now without worrying about rushing off to war. You know my heart; one more battle, one more war, one more time for the *Gipper.* It was easy to follow him once before. Some young person will fill the place I should have been, and I pray to God that He sends them all back home again safe.

"The one concern of the devil is to keep Christians from praying. He fears nothing from prayerless studies, prayerless work, prayerless religion. He laughs at our toil, mocks our wisdom; but he *trembles* when we pray!"
Samuel Chadwick (1840—1932)
English Methodist Theologian

Therefore, beloved, looking forward to these things,
be diligent to be found by Him in peace,
without spot and blameless;

2 Peter 3:14

"Neither do I condemn you;
Go and Sin No more"

John 8:11

Suggested Readings

The Holy Bible, also on sound track in dramatic form
Declaration of Independence, The United States of America
Constitution, The United States of America

Peter Schweizer, Reagan's War, for a detailed perspective on just how desperate it all was, and how we won the Cold War.

Alice Rains Trulock, In the Hands of Providence, for a detailed analysis and very readable account of one of America's brightest heroic stars of our Civil War, Joshua L. Chamberlain.

Doris Kearns Goodwin, Team of Rivals, for a detailed account of Abraham Lincoln's miraculous administration of our young nation's most terrible hour.

Ralph Ketcham, James Madison, biography of our fourth president. Brilliant expose' on the creation of our constitutional form of republican government.

David McCullough, John Adams, biography of a nation builder. Our First Vice President and Second President will astound the reader with facts about his forgotten legacy.

Walter Isaacson, Benjamin Franklin, biography to define the American mind and spirit. In-depth insight into the life of one of our greatest American founders.

Joseph P. Ellis, Founding Brothers, treatise on seven American founders who would transform a continent and the world.

David McCullough, <u>1776</u>, an account of the fateful year rendering concise and illuminating perspective into George Washington's leadership and the American struggle for independence.

Russell F. Weigley, <u>The American Way of War</u>, a history of American military strategy and policy up through the Vietnam war.

Carl Von Clausewitz, <u>On War</u>, classic expression on human armed conflict, strategies and tactics.

Michael and Jeff Shaara, <u>The Civil War Trilogy</u>, historical fiction of our American Civil War. Currently Two movies based on these works, "Gettysburg" and "Gods and Generals."

<u>One Hundred and One Famous Poems</u>, my edition is from 1926, but it is still available under this title. Marvelous compilation of many traditional poets you will enjoy.

Walter Isaacson, <u>Einstein: His Life and Universe</u>, presents a very readable account of the once unknown genius who often contradicts himself and common sense.

"God does not play dice [with the universe]."
Albert Einstein
(1879 - 1955)
Theoretical Physicist and Philosopher

"Einstein, stop telling God what to do."
Niels Bohr
(1885-1962)
Danish Physicist and Philosopher